Contents

*

Foreword by Jen Hatmaker

*

Every so often, a writer comes along that hits this perfect bull's-eye of communication. Hand to the heavens, Sarah Bessey is one of them. She manages to be poetic but still accessible, prophetic but still gentle, crazy smart but still approachable, strong but still gracious. I have no idea how she does it, but at the end of *Out of Sorts*, I basically wanted to curl up into every single paragraph and stay there forever.

I'll tell you what: this is the Jesus I know and love, the one Sarah describes. This is the church I crave, the one she found. Like Sarah, I have also taken a meandering spiritual voyage, and with the trustworthiness of a good leader and the kindness of a good friend, she laid out a clear path through the melee. Like a cold glass of water on a scorching day, she gave permission to struggle, to doubt, to leave, to come back. What a gift! I would have given anything to have this book in my hands when I was in my own wilderness. Even years later, it still set me free from leftover confusion I've been carrying around like a burden I didn't feel allowed to drop. I read every word of this book and laid it all down once and for all.

Because here is the Good News that Sarah never deviates from, never muddies, never gets out of order: Jesus remains. He is worth it all. He is under the steeples and in the wilderness. He is in the megachurch and in the spiritual conversation at the bar. He inhabits our certainty and also our doubt. He is every good thing that ever was or will be, and He is still in the business of saving our lives. Really, that's the thing. It is our hope and salvation, and everything else is just details. The longer I live, the clearer this becomes. (The way Sarah talks about Jesus in *Out of Sorts* will undo you. The entire book is like a love letter.)

When I got to this paragraph, I underlined it and high-lighted it then circled it in case my eyes were not yet convinced to return to it again and again:

> I hope we all wrestle. I hope we look deep into our hearts and sift through our theology, our methodology, our praxis, our ecclesiology, all of it. I hope we get angry and that we say true things. I hope we push back against celebrity and consumerism; I hope we live into our birthright as a prophetic outpost for the Kingdom. I hope we get our toes stepped on and then forgive. I hope we become openhearted and open-armed. I hope we are known as the ones who love.
>
> I hope we change. I hope we grow. I hope we push against the darkness and let the light in and breathe into the kingdom come. I hope we become a refuge for the weary and the pilgrim, for the child and the aged, for the ones who have been strong too long. And I hope we all live like we are loved.

I hope we all live like we are loved. Full stop. I can tell you this because Sarah is my actual, in real life, sincerest of friends: this is how she truly lives and leads. She is leading me right now, and I couldn't be more grateful. Sarah has taught me that deconstruction has its place, and there is holy permission to lean into it. She has also taught me that the rebuilding and reclaiming is sacred territory, and it is noble work that heals. (Sarah, how lovely to not feel alone in the process; thank you, friend. Your presence in my life is an unimaginable blessing.)

What an exciting time to be a part of the body of Christ! What leaders we have! What freedom we claim! God is working liberation throughout His people, and His kingdom is coming in so many astonishing ways. This is the only generation of the Church we will ever be a part of, and I am incredibly thankful to labor alongside such faithful, brave, beautiful believers.

Listen, Wanderer, Wonderer, Church Girl, Question Asker, Status-Quo Upender, those of you in the in-between some-where, those of you in the wilderness, those of you safely home: this book will be a balm. If you have ever trusted me, now is the time. What you will find in these pages is nothing short of a gift. There are plenty of us out here reimagining, rethink-ing, reevaluating, restarting. You aren't alone. Sit down, pour yourself a cuppa tea (I'm channeling Sarah here), and receive this permission to leave behind the stale trappings of religion in order to find Jesus again. He is as good as we ever hoped. Thank you, my dearest Sarah Bessey, for helping us find our way back home.

1

Out of Sorts

A BEGINNING

Once upon a time, you had it all beautifully sorted out.

Then you didn't.

* * *

Out of Sorts: a state of being in one's heart or mind or body. Often used to describe one's sense of self at a time when you feel like everything you once knew *for sure* has to be figured out all over again.

Nothing feels quite right. Nothing is quite where it belongs anymore. Everything moved . . . or maybe you moved. Either way, you feel disoriented.

Then: "How's your walk with God these days, sister?"

"Oh, glory to glory, brother! I'm blessed and highly favored!"

Now: "How's your walk with God these days, sister?"

"Oh, it's . . . I'm . . . a bit . . . out of sorts."

At sixes and sevens. Bewildered. Baffled. Caught between what-was and what-will-be. Walking away from something, perhaps, but not quite sure where you're even headed.

* * *

This book isn't an argument to make or a point to take. It isn't a single story with a plot and a climax and a denouement, and it doesn't have a simple three-step program to follow with nicely spaced headers.

I don't think this book will be turned into a calendar for the gift shop.

It's about loss and how we cope with change. It's about Jesus and why I love Him and follow Him. It's about church and church people and why both make me crazy but why I can't seem to quit either. It's about embracing a faith, which evolves, and the stuff I used to think about God but I don't think anymore, and it's about the new things I think and believe that turned out to be old. It's about the evolution of a soul and the ways I've failed; it's about letting go of the fear and walking out into the unknown.

It's about the beautiful things we might reclaim and the stuff we may decide to kick to the curb. It's a book about making peace with unanswered questions and being content to live into the answers as they come. It's about being comfortable with where we land for now, while holding our hands open for where the Spirit leads us next. It's about not apologizing for our transformation and change in response to the unchanging Christ.

It's about not apologizing for our transformation and change in response to the unchanging Christ.

Really, it's a book about not being afraid. This book is my way of leaving the light on for the ones who are wandering.

* * *

I've heard that most of our theology is formed by autobiography. This is true in my case and maybe it's true for you too.

I think that is why I love reading or hearing other people's stories of faith—the conversion, the wrestling, the falling away, the calling, the triumphs, the tenderness, the questions, the why behind all of it. I feel like I'll know Jesus better if I hear about how you love Him or how you find Him or how you experience the divine in your life. Emily Dickinson wrote,

> *Tell all the truth, but tell it slant—*
> *. . .*
> *The truth must dazzle gradually,*
> *or every man be blind.*[1]

Come at it sideways, let me hear the truth, but let the truth find me too. We're all still being slowly dazzled.

* * *

I am still wrestling with some aspects of my Mother Church. Perhaps you are too. Resting in the in-betweens is okay for now. You may find, like me, that you are reclaiming more and more, fighting your way through the weeds of over-realization or extreme cases or weirdness or wounding, to find the seed of the real that is still there. After the fury, after the rebellion, after the wrestling, after the weighing and the sifting and the casting off and putting on, after the contemplation and the wilderness—after the sorting—comes the end of the striving and then comes rest.

Søren Kierkegaard said, "It is perfectly true, as philosophers say, that life must be understood backwards. But they forget the other proposition, that it must be lived forwards."[2]

Perhaps we are never really free from the ones who came before us; we simply make our peace with the ways they haunt us still.

* * *

A while ago, a new friend, Nadia, drove me to the airport in Denver after a conference. We spoke of the power of resurrection in our lives, how the very things that used to hurt us were instruments of our healing. We talked about all the ways that our lives had been changed, how our eyes had been opened, how our worlds had been made new because of this man from Nazareth.

"Look at us!" I was laughing through my tears. "What in the world? It's like we've been born again, all over again!"

That's when Nadia told me that it was a real thing. She called it the "second naiveté." And she said, "That's us. We're naive all over again. By choice."

Nadia was referencing the work of French philosopher Paul Ricoeur. Ricoeur thought we began our lives in the first naiveté: basically, we take everything we are taught at face value. Some of us never move out of this stage in our spiritual formation and growth. We simply stay faithful to what we were taught at the beginning. But most of us, at some point, will encounter the second stage, which he called "critical distance." This is the time in our formation when we begin to . . . well, doubt. We begin to question. We hold our faith up to the light and see only the holes and inconsistencies.

In a modern world, few of us can escape a logical look at

our faith without some serious intellectual dishonesty. A lot of what our ancient-future religion teaches doesn't hold up to modern logic. Many of us simply stay in this rational stage, and sadly, when we become rational, some magic and beauty is lost to us.

Yet he writes, "Beyond the desert of criticism, we wish to be called again."[3] I remember crying out to God once while in the midst of what I called my wilderness, what Ricoeur calls the critical distance, because I was longing to "go back." It was somehow easier when life and faith and God were an exercise in rule making and literalism, in black-and-white cause and effect. I found it was not enough to live without the magic and the beauty, without the wonder. I couldn't return to my first naiveté and I missed the simplicity of it. I wanted to be called again, to hear the voice of God again, perhaps never more wildly than when it felt like the God I once knew was disappearing like steam on a mirror.

But those who continue to press forward can find what Ricoeur called a second naiveté. I didn't know it, but I was pressing through my wilderness to deliverance, toward that place on the other side of rationality, when we reengage with our faith with new eyes. We take responsibility for what we believe and do. We understand our texts or ideas or practices differently, yes, but also with a sweetness because we are there by choice. As Richard Rohr writes, "the same passion which leads us away from God can also lead us back to God and to our true selves."[4]

In my own journey, I witness this trajectory: the first naiveté of my faith, then the bitter struggle and relief in the critical distance, and now, a second, sweet naiveté.

The second naiveté is life after the death of what was once so alive, after the sorting through what remains, after the rummage sale perhaps. We have an inheritance that we have care-fully curated.

No wonder Nadia and I were crying in the car. We had sorted through our faith. We were still tossing what needed

We have an inheritance that we have carefully curated.

to be thrown out and reclaiming what needed to be treasured. We had found beauty and pain were threaded together. We were choosing this life, this Jesus, over and over again.

* * *

I've come to believe that there is always a bit of grief to the sorting out of a life, to making sense of the stories and the moments and intersections, in our ability to move forward with integrity. We figure out what we need to keep, what we need to throw away, and what we need to repurpose. Sometimes what looks like junk becomes precious because of the memories it holds. Other times, the memories are painful, and so we hold them to remind ourselves: *never again.* But as we make small piles of treasures and trash, we are sorting through a life and through our grief, making the way clear to move forward. This happens when someone we love dies, you know. We remember the person's life and we sort through our grief, our memories, our experiences, so we can find a way to move forward.

For instance, I clearly remember sitting in my maternal granny's hospital room while she was dying. I was curled up in one of those plastic-covered hospital chairs in the corner, five months pregnant with my eldest daughter. We granddaughters took turns in that room, ostensibly there to offer our mothers a respite. In reality, while the respite was offered, they never took us up on it: they never left her side.

One afternoon, I sat in that chair with a Styrofoam cup of tepid Red Rose tea in my hand. Red Rose is the tea of hospitals, funerals, and church basements. My mother sat on one side of her mother's bed; her older sister sat on the other. They never moved as the last hours stretched out. They simply sat in her presence, holding her hands while she slept within the morphine, ticking the clock toward death. I watched them minister to her and to each other in silence. They would catch eyes sometimes, and I knew an entire conversation was happening between them across that bed. The sisters were waiting, but they were waiting in peace.

Later that day, my granny's husband of ten years, her late-in-life love, crawled into her bed with her. Owen curled around her while she slept away from us, and he held her close till nearly her last breath.

She died, and we all felt the peace of it.

After she died, her children gathered in her apartment. Owen gave them the gift of space to sort things out and to remember. My granny didn't have much worldly treasure: she lived on an old-age pension in a tiny apartment in Edmonton. Humble or not, that final sort-through after death is a place of reckoning and it's an altar.

They stayed up through the night, reconnecting with their mother by telling the stories of her things, choosing items for themselves and assigning gifts to the grandchildren. My mother came home with a box of Granny's things, but she couldn't bring herself to really sort through it for quite a while. The grief was still too new. That box sat in the basement. When she was ready to sort through, it was there waiting. In the meantime, she began to learn how to live without her mother.

A year after the funeral, we met up at my auntie's house for

Easter weekend. We looked at old pictures. We told the stories to each other so we would remember; we each had such different experiences of her, we needed to share our narratives to gather the full complexity of her life. We even talked about her things and what we had done with them, how they traveled with us through our lives and where they lived in our homes.

Later that night, when everyone else had gone home, I tucked my then six-month-old daughter into her fold-and-go bassinet in the guest room. I stayed up too late, sitting on the couch beside my mother and her sister with a recently discovered box of old letters, receipts, and scraps of photos. They went through them, sometimes laughing, sometimes crying, sometimes angry or sad. They passed the bits of paper and photographs to me: *Hold this one*, they said. *And this one. Remember this? Oh, let me tell you about this one!* It was their instinct to fill in the blanks for me, to help me see the truth of their mother, to love her better because of how they had loved her.

Sometimes our most holy calling is to listen, to bear witness.

I didn't say much that night; sometimes our most holy calling is to listen, to bear witness. I held the scraps and the stories of what remained from the sort, my legacy.

* * *

But we weren't given the gift of sorting when my dad's mother passed away.

My grandma Nellie wasn't a typical grandmotherly type: she was tall and strong, hardworking and opinionated, ferocious and kind. She felt things deeply, yet she experienced grief and devastating loss with the prairie stoicism of the time. She loved hockey and gardening and western novels; she'd rather be out-doors than in any lovely room. We wrote letters throughout my life; I have them all saved in a shoebox still. It's probably silly to dare imagine that I understood her at all, but I tried. And she loved me well. When I was young, I worshipped her. Even later when the spell broke, I always felt at home in her stern love.

One day, when I was about seven years old, I was riding with Nellie and my grandpa Ken in his old red-and-white Chevy truck on our way to our shared family cottage. We were out of range of the radio, and the windows were rolled down because it was a stifling day. Even the wind was hot in my hair. I was feeling sleepy, content as only a secure child can feel. I leaned my head against her warm arm, so my ear was pressed right against her bare skin, and she was humming wordless melodies. The reverberations in her skin wound down into my own body. I remember wishing I could stay there, in that spare truck cab, smelling of my grandpa's cigarettes and her perfume and my suntan lotion, forever. This is also how we absorb our legacies, slowly over time, through presence and osmosis.

* * *

My father is estranged from one of his brothers, and despite his efforts at reconciliation, the great sorrow remains part of our story. Even when their mother was dying, they were un-reconciled. My father remains deeply grieved at their broken relationship, but he respects it. At some point, we all have to let people live their lives, even if that means they want to live them far away from us. And it was quite clear that my uncle, believing in the truth of his reasons, had no wish to live his life in any sort of contact or familial friendship with any of us.

History repeats itself. This broken bond of brothers happened, yes, but I could argue that it was always going to happen, that it was our legacy. My father's own uncles—Nellie's brothers—lived and died in decades of silence. They grew old on the same family farm and willfully became enemies, then remained strangers in their pride. They died unreconciled. So when estrangement reemerged in my father's generation, we all knew that—barring a miracle—there would be no happy ending. There would be no forgiveness. Once the grudge begins, it never ends. Maybe we're all just corkscrewing around the same stories over the years.

Things like this are bearable in a regular day-to-day life, but they become unbearable when shadows fall. So even though the family was splintered, it was mostly okay, bearable, for all of us as we got on with our separate lives, right up until Nellie began to die in good earnest.

* * *

I still firmly believe Nellie died because she simply made up her mind to do so. She was ready for death, and so death came at her bidding. Her end-of-life care instructions were clear, without sentimentality. If it was time to die, then for mercy's sake, let's get on with it.

Nellie grew up on the prairies of Canada. Life wasn't easy, but she belonged there. Not all women do, we knew that well, but she did—she was a survivor. She was born in the Roaring Twenties but her story was not a scene out of *The Great Gatsby*. There in the land of the living skies, the Twenties roared with work. Tiny farmhouse, a father who battled with alcoholism, Canadian winters—so much labor required to simply survive. Her family made their own bread, churned their own butter, milked the cows, raised a vegetable garden, and "did down" the vegetables and fruits (which is what we call canning and preserving), so they'd have food when the winter came. She attended a one-room schoolhouse until grade eight and then had to take correspondence courses for grades nine and ten. She loved to learn and longed to be a teacher but it was not to be. She told me once that she cried every night for weeks over the death of that dream.

Nellie wasn't beautiful for any era: her bones were too sharp, her height too commanding, her face too long, her straightforward gaze too intimidating. But she was self-possessed, taking the loneliness of her landscape into her heart, content to stand. They said she rode horses like a man. She would put on her slacks and race with the boys, defying everyone just to feel the wind on her face.

When she moved to the city with her new husband after the war, she missed the farm. If she had been a boy, she might never have left her homestead. But instead, she found herself married to a local boy whose greatest charm was a gift for gab. She raised their three boys and buried a stillborn daughter, making a home in the postwar bungalows of Regina and faithfully working the complaints desk at Simpson Sears department store.

But her longing for freedom was always there: when you grow up under the stars of the prairie and the wild winds, it's hard to submit to the city, I imagine.

When I was a kid, my uncles and my father used to tell stories about her that made me howl with laughter. When she wanted a cellar under the house, and her husband, Ken, kept putting it off, she grabbed a shovel and simply dug it out herself. When neighborhood toughs picked on her kids, they found themselves on the receiving end of her sharp tongue and never dared again. When a big dog chased her boys and terrorized the neighborhood, she grabbed up a two-by-four and chased that dog right back up the street to his yard. By the time she was finished with the dog and its owner, both were on their best behavior. Nellie's entire parenting philosophy can be summed up in one sentence: "No child is going to be the boss of me."

To me, Nellie embodied the prairie we loved. At times, hard and indomitable, but at others, caressing, beautiful, and tender. I worshipped her when I was a child, yes, but I grew to love her all the more for her complexities, her vastness, her sweeping presence, her edges. She was never simple or trite; I am unable to sum her up by the usual grandmotherly platitudes.

When she died, some little-girl part of me couldn't believe it. How could such a strong woman, so resolutely alive, be dead?

* * *

She died. And the family did not gather for the sort. We didn't get to go to her house and tell stories about our favorite photos or treasures, swapping memories to help us say good-bye. We simply waited in a hotel room while my uncle took care of all the details. Our grief had no release of storytelling and memory keeping. No books and costume jewelry and dusty boxes of black-and-white photos to mull over. We needed to laugh so we could welcome the tears. We needed to sort through her life, together, and we needed to take care of the details together. Instead, we went to the funeral home for her wake on the night before her burial. We stood in the heavy room, drinking Red Rose tea, awkward and silent strangers to one another. How do you hug someone, offer comfort to someone who won't speak to you?

I had asked my dad to request a box since we weren't going to her house to sort her things out together. After the funeral, my uncle presented me with a cardboard box from her house containing a few scrapbooks of her newspaper clippings, a couple of letters I had written to her, random knickknacks. It was a casual smattering, but it was beautiful to me. At least it was something.

I do have a few of Nellie's things, and I'm forever thankful for those treasures. In the years before her death, every time I visited—which wasn't often, since I lived far away—she would fill my suitcase with her chipped teacups and saucers, dusty cardboard hardback westerns by Zane Grey, a few pieces of costume jewelry, and other tchotchkes. In my dining room cabinet, I have her decorative plate imprinted with gold-leafed wheat stalks and the prayer "Give us this day our daily bread"; it used to sit in her dining room cabinet. I have her tiny orange ceramic cat, tail curled around its slender body. It used to sit on her kitchen windowsill, presiding over the grandkids washing dishes.

Later, I heard that my estranged uncle held an estate sale to dispose of her things. I didn't go to the sale because I wasn't invited or informed until it was over. Whatever she had given me before her death was all I had now.

Every once in a while, nearly ten years later, I remember something of hers and I wonder what happened to it. What happened to the mirror that hung in the entryway? What happened to the midcentury bread box? The candy dishes that sat on the coffee table? The little ceramic animals hiding among the leaves in her African violets from the front room? Where are her things?

It's hard to move forward when you feel like you never properly said good-bye or resolved your memories. Someone else bought most of her things, and whatever was left went to the Salvation Army to sit on metal shelves under fluorescent lights, examined by the uninterested. I wonder now if the experience of sitting together, telling the stories as we sorted through her home, if that would have healed us? If we needed to learn to love each other better by all loving the same old woman?

* * *

We sort on the threshold of change; it's how we gather the courage to eventually walk through the door and out into the new day's light. Of course there is grief in this process, whether it's from the death of a loved one or the death of an old way of life. Of course there is.

Whether it's in our relationship with God or with our own families, at some point we find that it is time to sort. It's time to figure out what we need to keep, what we need to toss, and what we need to reclaim. And we need to tell our stories in order to move forward.

Every ending is also a new beginning.

> *Whether it's in our relationship with God or with our own families, at some point we find that it is time to sort.*

* * *

Every five hundred years or so, the Church has a big rummage sale. Phyllis Tickle is the theologian who introduced me to the idea of the holy rummage sale. She credits it to an Anglican bishop named Mark Dyer, who once quipped that "about every five hundred years the Church feels compelled to hold a giant rummage sale."

Tickle is of the opinion that the Church is on the edge of a great shift: she calls it the Great Emergence. She writes "about every five hundred years the empowered structures of institutionalized Christianity, whatever they may be at that time, become an intolerable carapace that must be shattered in order that renewal and new growth may occur."[5]

First there was the establishment of the Church. Then in the sixth century, we experienced the fall of the Roman Empire, or the dawn of the Dark Ages in Christianity (it can be said that this was the bright season of other religions, such as Islam, which enjoyed great growth in theology, science, literature, and art during our Dark Ages). Then roughly five hundred years later, we experienced the Great Schism, when the ancient Church split into the East and West. After another five hundred years, we experienced the Great Reformation. Now we are creeping resolutely toward another "great" disruption. It's simply part of our life cycle as Christians. The old remains in some form or another, but the new expression will launch the Church into a new world. Tickle explains that every time the incrustations of an overly established Christianity have been broken open, the faith has spread—and been spread—dramatically into new geographic and demographic areas, thereby increasing exponentially the range and depth of Christianity's reach as a result of its time of unease and distress. Thus, for example, the birth of Protestantism not only established a new, powerful way of being Christian, but it also forced Roman Catholicism to change its own structures and praxis. As a result of both those developments, Christianity was spread over far more of the earth's territories than it ever had been in the past.

So right now, we are all cleaning out our homes. We are in a time, much like the Great Schism and the Great Reformation, of sorting through our religion as a universal Church. It's a fascinating study to look at how we've landed here: technology, philosophy, science, medicine, art, sexuality, politics, ethics, faith, media, development, globalization. The Church is being reinvented in response. We are dying, perhaps, but even death is part of our story: it comes right before resurrection.

It's already happening globally—on the margins and among the disenfranchised, in the outsiders and the grass roots. I'm sure the great bastions of power and leadership within the Church are feeling the strain of the shift.

> *We are dying, perhaps, but even death is part of our story: it comes right before resurrection.*

* * *

This got me to thinking: If the Church is in the midst of a rummage sale, aren't we all in the midst of a rummage sale?

With all the hand-wringing about the state of the influence and power of the Church in society, I wonder if we've forgotten that the Church isn't simply an institution. It's us. We're it. We are all standing in our own homes, looking at all the boxes and the junk and the treasures of our inheritance, and we are thinking to ourselves, "God, what a mess. Someday I really need to do something about all this."

* * *

We sort through our mess on the threshold of change, don't we? When we are moving. When there has been a death. When someone leaves. When we need the space. When we are changing in some way. Even if we're glad to be getting rid of things, there is still an emotional attachment to our stuff that plays out as we figure out what needs to stay and what needs to go.

After their parents died, my own parents decided to get their house in order. Rather than leaving us with a houseful of receipts and boxes of unidentified people in photos and scraps of bank statements to follow like a trail of breadcrumbs, they embarked on a several-year project of cleaning, purging, and organizing their home and their finances, even their decisions about death. They did not want to saddle my sister and me with the decisions about their end-of-life care or unorganized finances or junk accumulated over a lifetime. As an act of love, they wanted even their death to be as easy on us as possible.

* * *

I think about Nellie's things now and again. The grief of being denied the opportunity to go through her earthly treasures with the eye of love and the tenderness of memory still stings. In fact, I hate it. I hate that strangers picked through her things, I hate the thought of her special, scrimped-for knickknacks marked with price tags, I hate that the little things she loved have disappeared. Mostly, I hate that the estrangement continues in silence.

* * *

At the threshold of any change, we are confronted with fear. This is a pretty natural response to the birth of new life. In childbirth, Dr. William Sears calls it the "fear-tension-pain cycle."[6] When a woman is in labor and first feeling pain, she often becomes afraid and then she naturally holds back or tenses up, but that response only causes more pain, and so she experiences even more fear, which leads to more pain and so on. It's a terrible cycle that can impede or slow down birth. To interrupt the cycle, midwives and doctors recommend that women surrender to what is happening in their bodies. Counter to our intuition, the solution is to lean into the pain.

As I write this, my fourth little baby is sleeping in her crib, only three months old. Well, actually she is my eighth baby. I've lost four babies before birth. So this isn't exactly dry philosophy to me: I understand new birth and creation as more than a metaphor. As I have given birth to my babies, I learned the truth of Dr. Sears's words for myself: the fear made the pain worse. It was only by releasing the tension, by embracing my fear and my pain, that I was able to lean into the work of my body and be delivered.

I have had to lean into the pain and grief of my faith as well. Often, when we are on the threshold of new life or new birth, there is first the labor and the work. We become afraid of the pain we feel, and so we tense up and hold back—but that only increases the pain. These days, it's the fear of "what if?" and of loss that rises up in me. Whether it is the pain of community or of how we understand the Church or of how we have lost Jesus or of what we think about hell or signs and wonders or suffering, the fear to engage with our evolution only worsens the pain. As for a caterpillar in the cocoon, it becomes more painful to stay within our tight home than to simply break free and unfold our new wings. We fight the very thing that is meant to free us. It is only by releasing ourselves, giving ourselves fully over to the pain, and riding its cleansing wave that we find new life.

* * *

So this is a book about how feeling out of sorts leads us to sorting it out. About our personal rummage sales, how we engage with our first naiveté about so many areas of spirituality, and how we find the critical distance and the doubts. And then, how we experience a second birth. I'm under no illusions that I'm finished—and I don't imagine you're finished either. I tend to think that we are never fully done with these stages. Someday we'll look back on these opinions or landing points and know that this was simply an embarking point of another kind. But this is the process; this is how it begins. As we walk through this sort together, I'll also tell you about my own rummage sale, the grief that came with the sorting, and the healing that was ushered in. What I had to weigh and discard and evaluate will be different than what you will have in your own house: we all have our own legacies and baggage, family heirlooms and hoarders. One thing this book is not about is convincing you to end up in the exact same place or opinions as me. How could that even happen, when we start from different places? As Paul wrote in Romans 12:2 (NLT), "Let God transform you into a new person by changing the way you think. Then you will learn to know God's will for you, which is good and pleasing and perfect." Yes, we are being transformed by the renewing of our minds, transformed in response to the weight and shaping of Christ in us.

There are many of us out here sorting, I think. This might be a small candle, but I'll set mine on the lamp stand and you can set yours there too—and maybe our glow will light the path for others.

There's Something About That Name

ON GETTING TO KNOW JESUS

This is the liturgy of my childhood:

Jesus, Jesus, Jesus,
There's just something about that Name.
Master, Savior, Jesus,
Like the fragrance after the rain.
Jesus, Jesus, Jesus,
Let all heaven and earth proclaim,
Kings and kingdoms will all pass away,
But there's something about that Name.[1]

I first became acquainted with Jesus through the songs of my tiny, happy-clappy childhood churches in the prairies of Canada. I sang "Oh, Lord, you're beautiful" surrounded by misfit disciples who were on a first-name basis with resurrection. I sang the old songs about the blood of Jesus making me white as snow.

Is it any wonder I loved Jesus so much?

* * *

If we are seeing our lives as a gigantic rummage sale, then it's time for a wander through the nooks and crannies of our old ways. If we are looking for ways to sort our beliefs, we need to start at the center of everything: Jesus. I'm sure at some point in my life I'll learn how to preach without crying at the mention of His name, but that day isn't here.

* * *

I grew up on the fringes of the Canadian neo-charismatic movement of the seventies and eighties. Church historians call it the Third Wave after the Pentecostal revival of Azusa Street in 1906, and then the charismatic movement of the sixties and seventies. My parents came to Jesus in their thirties during that Third Wave in a turn-your-life-upside-down sort of way, bringing me and my sister with them into the strange new world of born-again Christians. Every area of Canada has a unique and complex relationship with religion—from the Mennonites in British Columbia and Manitoba to the Dutch Reformed communities of Ontario to the Catholics of Quebec. But we were the post-Christian, Anglo-Saxon prairie kids: suspicious of religion and the Establishment, opinionated on everything from politics to hockey, and our highest value was practicality. Religion had no dominant role in our family or community; the language of faith had disappeared from among us. There were occasional family members, like my great-grandmother, who still went to the United Church, but for most of us—to my memory and experiences anyway—religion and church simply didn't figure into the equation of real life. I'm sure now that there must have been Christians around me—perhaps a teacher, maybe a couple of fellow students, surely someone in our neighborhood—but at the time, they were invisible to me.

The only Christians I knew were the Peters family. They were my granny's neighbors across the alley. My first and primary understanding of Christians was this Mennonite family: they still hung their wash out to dry, grew gigantic gardens, and canned the bounty for homegrown feasting all year round. They kept bees and fished and worked with wood. They were warm and homey, kind and practical and peaceful. Their four teenage daughters were beautiful and wholesome. Their mother, Sara, became our family babysitter while my mother worked part-time, and we loved her even though—or perhaps because—she was so strict. If we did not like our tomato soup for lunch, she calmly allowed us to be excused from the table. But when we showed up a few hours later asking for a snack, that same bowl of tomato soup would be warmed up and placed before us to finish.

My mother's childhood had been far from stable, so now it makes perfect sense to me that she was drawn to Sara Peters and her capable motherliness. In fact, it was Sara's eldest daughter, Leila, who planted the seed in our family that led to our conversion. For Christmas one year, she gave us the *Bullfrogs and Butterflies* record.[2] My sister and I loved it; records were a real novelty for us. We memorized the songs and played it constantly. But while we were away at the little elementary school across the back alley, my mother would sit beside our record player, listening to the songs about how nothing compared to loving God, and how we can pray and be heard by God, about how bullfrogs and butterflies have both been born again. And she would cry and cry and cry. It was the first time she had heard the Gospel.

I think my mother saw the Peters family and thought: I need that. I need that kindness, that patience, the peace that exists in that home and in that woman. She longingly stood before their way of life as before a door closed to her. She heard the songs of the record and the key turned in the lock, the door to faith swung open. She leaped across the threshold.

* * *

When we became Christians, it was exactly in the way that charismatics become Christians: messy, experiential, consuming, and demonstrative. Our hearts were moved within us. We weren't academics. We weren't intellectuals. We weren't social justice activists. We weren't thinking of anything or anyone but ourselves and our desperation.

We were walking in darkness, and the Holy Spirit called us into the light of salvation. We were dead, and then we were alive. It sounds weird to write it all out like that, but I can't figure out another way to say it.

We were dead, and then we were alive.

Maybe I'm tired of finding other ways to say it, to make it more palatable and reasonable and logical.

What is this life in Christ like if not a bit of disorderly resurrection?

* * *

Jesus was real to us in those early days. Instead of calling our habit of reading the Bible "morning devotions" or "quiet time," we called it "spending time with Jesus." We spoke easily of Jesus, as if He was there with us, in our midst.

"What is Jesus telling you about this?" we would ask each other during times of conflict or confusion. The songs that rose to the rafters of the school gymnasiums and the community centers where we met were almost all simple love songs to Jesus. To us, Christ was the cord that bound us together, the reason for our resurrection, the north star, the center, the foundation. Some churches focus on memorizing the Bible, some on learning fine points of doctrine. Others gather for the cause of justice and mercy, others for political purposes. Our simple center was the man from Galilee.

To us, Christ was the cord that bound us together, the reason for our resurrection, the north star, the center, the foundation.

So yes, Jesus was part of our family, but at the same time, Jesus placed demands on us. Our lives changed thoroughly and completely. We adjusted our sails for Jesus, changing our habits, our thoughts, our words, our entertainment, our opinions to better fall in step with Him. We had no illusions; we knew we desperately needed to change. And we wanted our lives to look like His life somehow.

I was a child, so my understanding was limited, but I look back on my parents' bold decision to follow Christ so wholeheartedly, and I admit that I marvel. Because it cost them, and yet they counted that all as joy. Right from the start, Jesus was more than enough.

It was an unprecedented sort of thing for us to "get religion" so thoroughly. I wonder now if that conversion might be the root of the family conflict that has unfolded over the past thirty years: maybe my father's family didn't know how to relate to the new man he so suddenly became.

Mary Oliver wrote that at some point in your life, you determine to save the only life you can save—your own.[3] Yearning for freedom, my parents broke with their past in every way they could. They were determined that some unhealthy practices and behaviors that had plagued our families for generations would not plague their children. Perhaps this act of defiance was seen as an act of criticism. Saving your own life can be perceived as leaving everyone else behind.

It makes me glad to remember those days now, however others might disdain them. We were earnest and sincere with our homemade felt banners that hung on our walls and extolled the names of Jesus: Lion of Judah. Lamb of God. King of Kings. Alpha and Omega. Lord of Lords. Mighty God. Prince of Peace. Emmanuel. Messiah. Redeemer. Wonderful Counselor. Savior.

Lion of Judah. Lamb of God. King of Kings. Alpha and Omega. Lord of Lords. Mighty God. Prince of Peace. Emmanuel. Messiah. Redeemer. Wonderful Counselor. Savior.

Our Jesus walked among us with ease and constancy.

* * *

So of course, I asked Jesus to come into my heart in those early days.

I have complex feelings now about the whole Romans Road method[4] of salvation, about making impressionable five-year-olds repeat certain words for assurance of victory over hell, even about our language of having a "personal Lord and Savior."

But I still remember how it felt when I was a kid—how I felt so close to Jesus, so safe in the knowledge of His presence. I think charismatics are our generation's mystics: we speak easily of the divine and move in an intimacy with the Spirit that seems excessive to others, I imagine. That ease came to me by osmosis or habit or cultural conditioning, perhaps even by the Spirit herself, who could say. However it came about, the truth is that the language of intimacy with the Spirit and with Jesus and with God is my mother tongue.

When I was seven, I used to sit in the front row of our church's few lines of folding chairs. I can see myself so clearly: skinny, freckled, with dishwater-blond hair, and utterly transcendent with the Spirit. My feet were rooted in the gym floor, but my soul was soaring. I would sing with my whole heart, my whole body extended, the sound of tambourines and women around me.

Even now, those old simple choruses are my midnight songs; these are the songs I sing when I am mindlessly humming as I rock my babies to sleep. When they are sick, I lie beside them, passing my cool hand over their hair, singing quietly that "as the deer panteth for the water, so my soul longeth after thee."[5]

I loved our music. I know it wasn't highbrow hymn making. I've heard more than a few folks make fun of our repetitive singing—myself included. We thought the Spirit couldn't really move until we'd sung the chorus at least seven times. We just kept singing until something changed.

* * *

Later in my life, Jesus was replaced with the Industrial Church Complex. It feels as if the more I moved into church culture, the less I heard about Jesus. We could go months and months of Sunday sermons on how to live our lives, how to "apply the Word" to our lives for Monday morning, and yet never hear the name of Jesus. We moved into mainstream churches and movements,

The more I moved into church culture, the less I heard about Jesus.

which have their benefits. For instance, there isn't much long-winded "prophecy time" and no dueling tambourines. Accountability for finances and pastoral integrity were a big plus. Church as a priesthood of all believers can be a bit of a mess sometimes. Oh, and the established evangelical churches had much better youth group events—burger-eating contests, a karaoke machine, and earnest clean-cut teenaged boys to kiss breathless, late at night behind the buildings at church camp.

* * *

Perhaps Jesus was a bit too wild for the Church.

It was easier to expound on Paul's letters, for instance. Ah, Paul, here was a finely tuned mind, a man of practicalities. Jesus probably didn't know that we had bills to pay, budgets to meet, programs to run, bylaws to discuss, deacons to nominate, culture to influence, public-opinion battles to wage, doctrine to parse, lines to draw in the sand to mark who was in and who was out.

It seemed one could be a Christian without being a disciple of Jesus.

Jesus became the stuff of childhood song lyrics. Church became a social club at times, then it became a burden to bear. I'll write more about Church later in the book, but for now, I'll just say this: I lost Jesus in there. It seemed one could be a Christian without being a disciple of Jesus.

* * *

There are a lot of Jesuses running around these days.

There is the Jesus who wants you to find a good parking spot at the mall. There is the Jesus invoked at music awards and the one raised like a flag to celebrate capitalism and affluence. There is the Jesus drawing lines about who is "in" and who is "out," and there is the Jesus on both sides of the picket lines. There is the one in the slums and the one in suburbia and the one in Africa and the one in America and the one in Calgary. There is the Jesus who told Mother Teresa to touch the lepers and love with her hands, the one who led the bravest and kindest of men and women all the way to the end, and then there is the Jesus who supposedly inspired manifestos of hate, crusades, murder, and wars. And then there is the Jesus who likes everything you like and hates everything (or everyone) you hate and is quite pleased with everything about you. (I like that Jesus best sometimes.)

We create Jesus in our own image, don't we? "It is always true to some extent that we make our images of God," wrote Brennan Manning. "It is even truer that our image of God makes us. Eventually we become like the God we create."[6]

* * *

In my twenties, I decided to stop being a Christian because I did not want to be associated with the Church.

But I was still fascinated with Jesus.

For some time, I had been growing disenchanted with the Industrial Church Complex. I found some solace in the emerging church and in the rediscovery—for me, anyway—of ancient church traditions and the broader Church. I found progressive, thoughtful, and brilliant people among Christians. But for me and the Bride of Christ? Well, it still felt like I was just hanging on to a relationship that had already ended.

When I made the decision to stop going to church and to stop calling myself a Christian, it didn't feel good. But there had been a long litany of abuses, burn-out, and exhaustion.

The trail of hurt people, wounded souls, and even dead bodies was too great. It weighed on my soul, and I felt tremendous grief. I couldn't align myself with this anymore.

I could no longer reason away or gloss over the systemic abuses of power, the bitterness, the bigotry and hypocrisy, the sexism and racism, the consumerism, the big business of church that was consuming people and spitting them out for the "greater good." Church became the last place I wanted to be. I didn't trust Christians. And I was tired of pretending that those things were not real.

But through it all, I somehow knew one thing: this wasn't Jesus. Maybe it's because of my childhood foundation, but I instinctively knew that this Industrial Church Complex was not the stuff of the Prince of Peace. Even as I grew more disenchanted with organized religion, I was still hanging on to the hem of his garment, begging for healing.

I instinctively knew that this Industrial Church Complex was not the stuff of the Prince of Peace.

"I don't think I can be a Christian anymore," I told my husband. I needed to separate from that word for a while; it felt too full of baggage and weight. I felt like it aligned me with people from whom I would rather separate.

I began to call myself a follower of Jesus, instead of a Christian. I don't know why I thought that was a big difference, but to me at the time, it meant something. False construct, a trick of language alone perhaps, but I needed the space it gave my soul.

Then came the day when it dawned on me that if I was going to call myself a follower of Jesus, I should find out what that meant. It sounds so silly to write it out, but that is actually what happened. One day I realized that for years I hadn't thought about Jesus much beyond "He's cool." If I was going to orient my life around some guy named Jesus, it had to be more than a rejection of Christianity as I understood it in my narrow context and experiences.

In *Is God to Blame?*, Greg Boyd writes,

> Jesus is the perfect expression of God's thought, character, and will. He is God's self-definition to us. We have seen that in Christ, God defines and expresses Himself as a God of outrageous love. He is for us, not against us. God also defines humans as undeserving people with whom He is nevertheless in love. *This* is the Word and image of the true God.[7]

To know Jesus is to know God. And I found myself saying, without knowing what it meant, that I wanted to be like Jesus. And to be honest, I was growing tired of defining myself by what I wasn't.

I started where most good Protestants start: the Bible. I made the decision to read only the Gospels for a while—the books of Matthew, Mark, Luke, and John.

* * *

Jesus was not what I expected. Not what I remembered. I had expected a comfortable wise man, someone saying nice things about being nice and kind to people. I think I expected a version of Jesus I had tricked out of my memory: comfortable, safe. Clearly I'd blurred the Jesus of my childhood with the real one of the Gospels.

* * *

Jesus. His name felt like every question and every answer. There was a strain of something like unearthly music to His name, and part of me still believes that my desire to be like Jesus was the Spirit's call—deep calling unto deep,[8] as the psalmist wrote.

My broken heart—cynical, jaded, frustrated, angry, wounded—somehow exhaled at every mention of His name.

* * *

I read through all of it. And then again. And then again. Sometimes Jesus confused me, and sometimes He made me angry. Sometimes I thought He acted like a bit of a jerk. Then I began to read what other people thought about Jesus. I began to realize that I didn't understand much about the times of Jesus or what His parables meant to the audience who was listening to Him, so I studied them. Sometimes I experienced moments of startling clarity. (Sometimes.) I didn't want to sing sweet songs about Jesus anymore. Who was this man?

One of my first moments of clarity came in the Book of Luke, chapter 6. I had been reading the Gospels for nearly a year already by then, studying them, soaking in them. In that one passage of Scripture, Jesus had done everything from preaching the Sermon on the Mount to subverting our understanding of the Sabbath to telling us to love our enemies and give our lives away.

The entire chapter is so full and rich and robust, you could pretty much camp there for the rest of your life and still have something to learn at the end of it. But that day, as I read chapter 6, I was, well, *angry*. I felt ripped off.

Because this Jesus, the one here in the pages of my Bible, the one who spoke in the red letters, the one I was yearning to know in my heart of hearts and walk behind every day—this Jesus was so different from all those other Jesuses. He wasn't in a tidy box. He wasn't the property of any one religion or denomination or belief system, or of a governmental system or a financial system or a lifestyle. He was bigger, wilder, and more wonderful than all of that. And it made me feel angry to realize it.

I was sitting at our kitchen table while reading, and my husband was working in the kitchen because he had just brought in a load of vegetables from the garden. He was innocently stacking cucumbers and kale when I slammed my Bible on the table and hollered, "I'd follow that guy!"

After Brian peeled me off the ceiling, we ended up having a good talk about why I felt so angry as I read something I loved. Because I did love it. This Jesus was the one I wanted to know; this was the one I wanted to love; this was the Jesus I wanted to follow. I knew in that moment I would never walk away from Him, that it was worth it to shape my entire life around Him—however weird that looked sometimes—and He was why I wanted to learn a new way to be a Christian.

I wanted to follow Jesus: not a way of thinking or a doctrine, not a sermon or a list of rules, not political affiliations and church denominations or a path to a shiny-happy life or anything like that. I wanted to follow Him and love Him, right to the end, wherever He led. It occurred to me on that day that if I got to know Him—really, truly know Him—I could perhaps begin to spot counterfeit Jesuses. There are Jesuses out there who are co-opted for every cause and argument, and these false Jesuses bastardize the message and misrepresent a man none of us really understands—and we all do the co-opting, for everything from power to money to the smug feeling of being right while everyone else is wrong. We all do it, progressives and conservatives alike. Jesus isn't our mascot and He isn't the magic word.

I found His words in Luke 6:43–44: "You don't get wormy apples off a healthy tree, nor good apples off a diseased tree. The health of the apple tells the health of the tree. You must begin with your own life-giving lives. It's who you are, not what you say and do, that counts. Your true being brims over into true words and deeds."

I read those words—"You must begin with your own life-giving lives"—and suddenly I understood why Mary spilled her most precious perfumes and soaked His feet with her tears, drying them with her hair. No wonder the Bible uses the word "immediately" to describe how quickly fishermen dropped their nets and livelihoods to follow the man from Galilee. One of the biggest gifts of that season of my life was revisiting the stories I thought I knew and discovering that really, I didn't know them at all.

The more I read the Gospels, the more I got it: no wonder we love the real Him when we meet Him. The more I met people who followed this Jesus, the more I understood why I felt ripped off: I had been a Christian for who knows how long, and yet I had not seen *this* Jesus. Where had He been all along?

* * *

This was when Jesus became the center of everything to me. I began to understand that if I wanted to see God, I needed to see Jesus. He was the image of God for us. Everything I didn't understand about the Bible and about the Church was now filtered through the lens of Christ. If Jesus came to show us what God is truly like, then perhaps there have been ways—so many ways—in which we have missed it. Myself included. We aren't so different from the people of Jesus' own time here on earth: He is not the king we expect.

* * *

Our Jesus showed us and taught us that God is not keeping score, not how we keep score, and that He lavishes His riches equally on everyone who shows up.[9]

* * *

Dallas Willard flat out said it: Jesus was smart. Not just nice, not just good, not just moral.

He is not just nice, He is brilliant. He is the smartest man who ever lived. He is now supervising the entire course of world history[10] while simultaneously preparing the rest of the universe for our future role in it.[11] He always has the best information on everything, and certainly on the things that matter most in human life. Let us now hear His teachings on who has the good life, on who is among the truly blessed.

If I believed Jesus was who He said He was, then He was worth following. No longer could I look at His teachings in Scripture—the words actually recorded as having come from Him—as mere suggestions. As He said in Luke 6, "Why are you so polite with me, always saying 'Yes, sir,' and 'That's right, sir,' but never doing a thing I tell you? These words I speak to you are not simple additions to your life, homeowner improvements to your standard of living. They are foundation words, words to build a life on."

I had thought that Jesus wasn't practical and was somehow

unacquainted with "real life," as I called it. Who could love their enemies? Who could bless those who curse them? Who could lay down his life so willingly? Who could think it was more blessed to give than to receive? Who could turn the other cheek? *Who?*

I realized that I had been rationalizing my disobedience and my lack of discipleship because I thought Jesus just didn't get how it was for us real people.

I was wrong.

I wasn't bringing Jesus into my life; He was welcoming me into His. As Brennan Manning puts it, "Jesus Christ has made Himself the vital center of the Christian life. Jesus is not only the heart of Christianity, He is the center of humanity and reveals to us what it means to be human."[12]

> *I wasn't bringing Jesus into my life; He was welcoming me into His.*

I was being called to become like Him. "We don't reduce Christ to what we are; he raises us to what He is," wrote Paul.[13]

* * *

Understanding turned to adoration. Following Him is turning me into a disciple. This helps me to believe in wondrous things.

Even now, whenever I preach, I always end up in John 15. It's one of my favorite passages of Scripture. Here, Jesus is speaking to those He loves, for one last time before enduring the Cross. I think these words matter deeply for our lives too. He tells us to abide in the Vine, that apart from Him we can do nothing. This has become the cry of my heart since reorienting my life to Jesus—*let me abide in love.* As Richard Rohr writes in *Eager to Love*, "This concept for remaining or abiding moves all religion out of any esoteric realms of doctrinal outer space where it has for too long been lost."[14]

* * *

It strikes me as funny that my faith journey started with an easy childish love that turned into an intellectual rational understanding of Jesus, which led me right back to where I began: a passionate love for my Jesus.

I thought I grew out of the flags and the happy-clappy Jesus-is-my-boyfriend songs, that I was too wise and smart for such sentimental things, but in my maturity now I want to shout out hallelujah and fling myself to the ground prostrate, in gratitude for dirt and little boys, for babies and the lines around my eyes, for Johnny Cash and pine trees at dusk, for the taste of cold water and the vineyard, for the piano and the ones from among us who stand to lead us out into the day singing.

As I sorted through what I thought I knew about Jesus, my intellectual, rational understanding of Jesus turned again to love. Even now, I know that I don't know Him as well as I will someday. I know there are blind spots and places of question and doubt. I question, and I am refined by the questions. And now, I can only repeat the words of Peter in John 21:17 right before He betrayed Jesus, "Lord, you know everything. You know that I love you."

* * *

After a long wander, I have found myself back in a school gymnasium, bathed in the presence of Jesus, with my hands up to the rafters. I'm not a skinny kid anymore, I'm one of the church mothers now with children at my side or balanced on my hips. I don't dance much these days, but I'm still singing it out loud:

> *Oh, Lord, you're beautiful*
> *Your face is all I seek*
> *And when your eyes are on this child*
> *Your grace abounds to me.*[15]

3

Everyone Gets to Play

ON THEOLOGY AND CHANGE

In the last chapter, I've written about reclaiming my passion for Jesus. About finding the parts of my faith and spirituality that had been too long neglected and how I've learned to repurpose and reuse them. But here's the other side: I have had to toss some stuff out entirely. I've had to build up a bonfire in my backyard and throw a few cherished beliefs and opinions right into the flames.

There is something so satisfying about watching an ugly lie burn away to ash.

* * *

Here are just a few questions about theology, Scripture, and doctrine I've had over the years (yours will be different): Was a six-day creation literal? What is the point of the whole "accepting Jesus into my heart" thing? If you don't say the words right, are you going to hell? By the way, what is hell? Is it real? And while we're at it, what's heaven? Why did Jesus have to die? Is the God of the Old Testament stories of genocide and tribal war the same God as Jesus? Why won't God heal my friend? My child? Me? Why are there so many kinds of Christians? Does God still speak today? Can I trust how the Bible came to me? Is the Bible literal, inerrant truth? I've heard that God is sovereign and that we have free will, but I don't understand either one or how they work together. Is God to blame for suffering? Does God choose who goes to heaven and who goes to hell? What is the purpose of church? What makes a church a church instead of just a bunch of people hanging out? What's the deal with communion? Baptism? Why are we here on earth? How do I figure out what God wants me to do with my life? Don't even get me started on the Book of Revelation.

I think I have answers for some of them now. But those might change too.

* * *

Robert Farrar Capon writes in *The Supper of the Lamb*, "There, then, is the role of the amateur: to look the world back to grace."[1] It's for this same reason that, while I love professional hockey like the NHL games, nothing gets Canada more excited than the world junior hockey tournament. There's something about a bunch of kids who play just for the love of the game that is so sweet to us. They're amateurs, sure, maybe not as skilled as the professionals, but oh, do we love to cheer them on.

John Wimber used to say, "Everyone gets to play."[2] The founder of the Vineyard movement of churches, He meant that everyone gets to minister, everyone gets to hear from God, everyone has a part to play in this church and in this world, everyone gets to speak life and healing, to pray and to serve, to lead and to follow. When it comes to the Kingdom of God, everyone gets to play.

In 1 Peter 2:9, Peter writes, "You are the ones chosen by

God, chosen for the high calling of priestly work, chosen to be a holy people, God's instruments to do His work and speak out for Him, to tell others of the night-and-day difference He made for you—from nothing to something, from rejected to accepted." That's us—we have all gone from nothing

When it comes to the Kingdom of God, everyone gets to play.

to something, from rejected to accepted. And so we are priests to one another, and for one another. We all get to play.

One of our final tin gods as a Church is the belief that not everyone gets to "do" theology. Unless you've been to seminary and have a lot of letters after your name, unless you're in full-time vocational ministry, your thoughts or experiences about God aren't considered as valid or trustworthy.

There are folks who believe that I—as a woman who hasn't been to seminary—can't possibly play with the big boys when it comes to theology. My opinions don't matter as much; my experiences with Scripture and church, life and the Spirit don't count.

But I still believe that everyone gets to play. I get to read theology and study the master thinkers and form my opinions. I get to be challenged and to challenge, even if I'm doing that work far from the ivory tower of the well-educated elite. (That'll be the western Canadian kid in me coming out: we have a lively horror of the elite.) Of course I grapple with these questions. What thinking person doesn't find themselves wondering? Theology belongs just as much to the rest of us—the mother folding laundry, the father coaching basketball, the university student studying to be a nurse, the construction worker, the artist, the refugee—as it does to the great scholars.

In Acts 4, Peter and John were brought before the religious

elite because they had been preaching the resurrected Christ. The disciples had just been to the temple, where they encountered a man crippled since birth. When the man asked them for money, Peter replied, "I don't have a nickel to my name, but what I do have, I give you: In the name of Jesus Christ of Nazareth, walk!" and pulled him to his feet! The man was immediately healed. Then Peter addressed the crowd with a rousing sermon about repenting and turning our faces to God. The religious elite promptly arrested them and threw them into jail. The rulers met with Peter and John to interrogate them, but Peter wouldn't back down, declaring (verse 12) that salvation comes in no other way than Jesus.

> They couldn't take their eyes off them—Peter and John standing there so confident, so sure of themselves! Their fascination deepened when they realized these two were laymen with no training in Scripture or formal education. They recognized them as companions of Jesus, but with the man right before them, seeing him standing there so upright—so healed!—what could they say against that? (verses 13–14)

Later on in the chapter, when the religious leaders and scholars threatened Peter and John, warning them to stop preaching about Jesus, they shot back, "We can't keep quiet about what we've seen and heard." (verse 20)

Theology is simply what we think about God and then living that truth out in our right-now lives. So theology matters, not as a vast scholarly exercise or a fun way to tie knots in each other, but because those ideas trace their way back to what we truly believe about the nature and character of God, which informs everything in our lives. The Spirit leaves evidence of one who had, as the religious leaders identified, "been with Jesus." Oh, I long for that! I long for my work and my witness to testify to Jesus Christ. Anytime we wrestle with our theology, with how we live out the hope of glory, with what we know or believe or think or even hope about our God, I pray that we will have that same boldness to testify, to bring healing, to speak the truth, to worship.

And God continued to use wise and learned men and women throughout Scripture. Look at Paul, who was so well educated and trained in religious thought. As he wrote to the church in Philippi, "You know my pedigree: a legitimate birth, circumcised on the eighth day; an Israelite from the elite tribe of Benjamin; a strict and devout adherent to God's law; a fiery defender of the purity of my religion, even to the point of persecuting the church; a meticulous observer of everything set down in God's law Book." And yet, he writes,

The very credentials these people are waving around as something special, I'm tearing up and throwing out with the trash—along with everything else I used to take credit for. And why? Because of Christ. Yes, all the things I once thought were so important are gone from my life. Compared to the high privilege of knowing Christ Jesus as my Master, firsthand, everything I once thought I had going for me is insignificant—dog dung. I've dumped it all in the trash so that I could embrace Christ and be embraced by Him. I didn't want some petty, inferior brand of righteousness that comes from keeping a list of rules when I could get the robust kind that comes from trusting Christ—*God's* righteousness. (Philippians 4:6–9)

I'm not against credentials—far from it! But as Paul said, they're not righteousness. Credentials are no replacement for knowing Christ. And when we encounter someone who knows Christ, well, that person gets to play, and we get to play with them!

Perhaps this is the danger of dualistic thinking—this is right, so this is wrong. We need to hold the "yes, *and*" more than the "either/or." Yes, we need scholars and academics, leaders and ministers. *And* we need people like me—low-church, untrained laity who are a bit sloppy at times—to grapple with the deep theological issues, bringing our stories, our wisdom, our experiences, our knowledge to the larger conversation. Everyone gets to play.

> *When we encounter someone who knows Christ, well, that person gets to play, and we get to play with them!*

In Matthew 11:25, Jesus prayed aloud, "Thank you, Father, Lord of heaven and earth. You've concealed your ways from sophisticates and know-it-alls, but spelled them out clearly to ordinary people. Yes, Father, that's the way you like to work."

We have much to learn from the ordinary people, from people on the margins, from people who experience God and life so differently from ourselves. I'm still a recovering know-it-all.

* * *

Some of our great frustrations have a hidden gift. It used to frustrate me that my tradition—the charismatic Pentecostalish movement—was on average quite suspicious of education. We were working-class and experiential. We were wary of education and the elite. Now I wonder if that was a bit of a backlash situation. Our personal experiences of the divine weren't welcome in the seminaries or other halls of education. Our emotions and made-up uneducated liturgy, let alone the whole tongue-talking ecstasies, were dismissed, so we turned around, said, *fine, never mind, we didn't want to be with your lot anyway.* We have gone from being the black sheep of the Church to being the fastest-growing segment of the Church worldwide, but we still harbor a suspicion that we're the outsiders. We have grown prideful and defensive in some instances, suspicious that education is a tool to steal our fire or our passion and zeal for the Lord.

(So imagine my surprise when my experiences with theology, literature, curiosity, and art were precisely what God used to draw me near, igniting in me a zeal and passion unlike any tongue-talking churchy worship experience revival party of my life thus far.)

If any among us wanted to be a leader, we had only to be "set apart" by the community, or claim to have heard from God that this was our path. This had its downfalls, let me assure you. We occasionally lacked nuance and full understandings. In some tribes, it meant literalism and biblicalism, it meant an over-realized eschatology, it meant that our view of God was often too small, limited to our immediate experiences and very plain readings of Scripture without full understandings of context and historical meaning.

But here is the great part: we all got to play. In order to play, we didn't have to leave our communities or be separated from the place that gave us life. We relied much more on the Spirit than on man. Our experiences mattered; we expected the Spirit to show up in a purity of heart. We felt free to come boldly.

So this happy-clappy mum from western Canada never felt intimidated by theology. I believed I could play too. The hubris of my tradition has stood me in good stead: I'm not scared off. I don't think that theology is above my pay grade, not yet anyway.

One of the great surprises of the Church is the space to ask questions. Sure, there are some places and communities where that isn't true; but in the Church overall, there is likely room for you—room to learn and change. And then to learn you're not alone. We have company for the journey. There is a long legacy of troublemakers and question askers; there's a lot more room than we think.

* * *

If our theology doesn't shift and change over our lifetimes, then I have to wonder if we're paying attention. The Spirit is often breathing in the very changes or shifts that used to terrify us. Grace waits for us in the liminal space.

We can be afraid to question. We are afraid that if we let ourselves question our theology or doctrines—the theology we developed or were given in our first naiveté—that we will be at risk. We're afraid it would mean that we don't value Scripture, that we are questioning authority. That it would open us up to becoming one of those wishy-washy folks who only read the parts of the Bible that suit them and ignore the rest. I think that motivation is pure-hearted and earnest, but now I also see that it can be utterly motivated by the fear of "What if?" We are afraid of our

> *If our theology doesn't shift and change over our lifetimes, I have to wonder if we're paying attention.*

questions, afraid of finding new answers, afraid of a new way of thinking about or living with or relating to God. What if it changes us? What if we go the wrong way? What if we find our way to the fabled slippery slope and tumble head long into the fall? What if what if what if?

Let's be honest: this sorting can be terrifying. We might lose something valuable to us: our certainty, our church, our community, our comfort, our current view of our self. There are consequences for new answers and new understandings. Just as there are consequences for trying to remain the same, there are consequences for changing: we're never neutral.

And yet there is something exhilarating about a slippery slope. And there is usually rest waiting at the bottom. There is something wondrous about flinging open the door to the thing that scares you

Let's be honest: this sorting can be terrifying.

and saying, Bring it on. Let's hop onto this toboggan and ride all the way to the bottom; let's see what we find.

When you feel afraid of going too far, remember these words of David:

Is there any place I can go to avoid your Spirit? To be out of your sight? If I climb to the sky, you're there! If I go underground, you're there! If I flew on morning's wings to the far western horizon, You'd find me in a minute— you're already there waiting! Then I said to myself, "Oh, He even sees me in the dark! At night I'm immersed in the light!" It's a fact: darkness isn't dark to you; night and day, darkness and light, they're all the same to you. (Psalm 139:7–12 MSG)

* * *

When we're sorting things out, when we dare to ask questions, sometimes someone will pat us on the head and say, "Well, you know, you need to have faith like a child."[3]

Pat, pat, pat, right on the head. Patronize, patronize, patronize, right on the soul. Just stop wondering, stop wrestling. You aren't supposed to be a grown-up in the kingdom, darling, you're supposed to be like a child and accept what you've been taught and stop asking questions. Trust the truth you've been given.

To which I now respectfully ask: I'm sorry, but have you ever been around a child for any amount of time?

Because let me tell you, kids ask a lot of questions.

My tinies ask questions constantly. They want to know where the Eiffel Tower is and why it's there and why don't my friends go to church and why can't I marry Daddy and what time is it in China and what colors make pink and do you want to hear this song and why does this bug tickle me and why did Jesus die on the cross and why can't I watch this show and why do I need to sleep and on and on and *on.*

There is a natural curiosity that is inherent to children.

I think it's a bit dishonest to use "Have faith like a child" as a way to shut a person down. Like, somehow, it means we're not supposed to wonder, we're just supposed to accept. Now that I have a house full of small humanity, I think I'm beginning to understand why Jesus would encourage us to have faith like a child.

They don't know. *And so they ask.*

We don't know. And so we ask.

The asking isn't wrong. The wondering isn't wrong. The

doubt isn't wrong. It's humbling to admit you don't know; it takes guts to ask and wrestle. The childlike quality isn't unthinking acquiescence: it's curiosity.

But here is the key of a child, the true wonder of childlike faith: They truly want to know. They're not asking to be cool or to push back on the establishment or to prove anyone wrong or to grind an ax or make a point without making a change. Tinies ask because they want an answer.

So I'm in agreement with the words—*have faith like a child*—even if I'm not in agreement with the usual sentiment behind it.

* * *

Be curious. Look behind the curtain, push against the answers, lean into the questions or the pain. As the psalmist wrote, fly on morning's wings to the far western horizon, God is already there.[4]

God isn't threatened by our questions or our anger, our grief or our perplexed wonderings. I believe that the Spirit welcomes them—in fact, leads among them and in them. We ask because we want to know, because it matters to us, and so I believe it matters to God. And sometimes the answers are far wider and more welcoming than we ever imagined; other times our answer is to wait in the question, and sometimes the answer is another question altogether.

God isn't threatened by our questions or our anger, our grief or our perplexed wonderings.

After all, in the Gospels, Jesus answered a lot of questions with more questions, pushing us to think in a new direction. It's interesting how often Jesus disrupted the comfortable—the ones who thought their answers were settled and done, the ones who were convinced that their righteousness was equal to their rightness. It's interesting how He poked and prodded, even how often He turned their answers around and moved them further into redemption than they were willing to go.

I still wrestle with theology. I grow in understanding; my answers evolve. Just when I think that this time I've settled something once and for all, I find a new angle or a new question arises or I read something that pushes against my answer—relationships, encounters with God and Scripture, circumstances even—and I'm left again, wondering. Perhaps this is the shift we're really talking about—not settling down on our answers, building temples their weight was never meant to hold.

The Spirit is part of the dance in me and for me. I find it exciting now, challenging. I know it makes some people uncomfortable. We want the Right Answer, once and for all. I think those things happen sometimes, absolutely, but my catalog of Right Answers grows smaller every year.

* * *

I've already referenced Ricoeur's stages, but another fascinating (okay, also very technical) study about our spiritual development came from James W. Fowler in *Stages of Faith: The Psychology of Human Development and the Quest for Meaning*.[5] After an extensive academic study, he summarizes the stages of faith using developmental milestones or ages. For instance, in the child stage of our faith, Fowler's Stage Two, we are "mythic-literal," which means that we take everything literally, even our metaphors. We can't always tell the difference between imagination and reality. We highly value predictable cause and effect. As I read about this stage, I saw some aspects of my former self: "If I pray this way, God will answer" or "If I am good, then I will have a good life" or "If I stand on the word of God, nothing bad will ever happen to me." In the adolescent stage, Fowler's Stage Three, we move into "synthetic-conventional," which means that we are conforming to authority, so anything that doesn't "fit" with the faith we've been given is rejected. Conflict is feared or ignored.

Fowler provocatively argues that our current way of doing church "works best" if we remain in this stage.[6] After all, this is the point of our journey where we obey authority, seldom question, are suspicious of challenge, or see anomalies to the expected script as a threat. It's telling that our faith communities are often structured not only for people at this stage of faith development but, in fact, often unwittingly work to ensure that we remain there.

We progress in stage four to angst and struggle, an openness to the conflicts and questions. I confess I have a tender spot for this stage of our development—perhaps because I started out being afraid of questions and struggle. It's a fearsome responsibility to examine our faith.

And as I said, we often experience this transition at the threshold of change, when there is a catalytic event or happening, so of course it comes with grief or anger. But as development continues, we move from this stage to one of acknowledging paradox and transcendence.

And finally, a few of us may land in the sixth stage: universalizing, when we come at last to compassion and love and grace, to the enlightenment of treating all with ferocious love and tender justice.

* * *

When I was preparing to leave home, my mother used to joke about "putting prickles in the nest." She had read somewhere that when the time comes for baby birds to learn to fly, the mother birds put sticks or thorns in their nests. By making the nest uncomfortable, the mother bird is actually giving her babies a gift: the gift of flight and growth. Discomfort causes the baby birds to embrace their fundamental self as one who takes wing. My mother wanted me to fly more than she wanted me to stay in the nest with my wings clipped forever. In our case, I was leaving home, moving to the United States in a time when phone calls home were expensive and rare and e-mail didn't exist for most of us; and so it was our first big "break" from each other. I was alternately thrilled and terrified at the freedom that lay before me. So when I faltered, she would put her own version of "prickles" in the nest. It became a bit of a joke between us, figuring out the discomfort of the between space of child and adult. Now I find myself wondering at times if the Spirit is the one putting prickles in our nests.

The Holy Spirit has been represented in Christian imagery, art, and Scripture as everything from fire to water, wind to oil, and of course a dove, each metaphor inadequate to describe the nature and character of God. But I remembered that phrase—prickles in the nest—when I was reading Fowler, and I had to chuckle. Maybe the Holy Spirit is more like a mother bird than we realize. To move us from one stage of faithful growth and development to the next, our nests, which used to be so com-

I find myself wondering at times if the Spirit is the one putting prickles in our nests.

fortable, must become uncomfortable to us. We outgrow them. And yet we need more encouragement to fly than we know. A few well-placed prickles from the Spirit serve to stretch our wings for the first time, perhaps.

* * *

Here is the other part: it's okay to hang on for a while. When I read through Fowler's work, I was struck by how often I revisited certain stages of my growth out of sheer willpower. I would perhaps move into a new stage, feel afraid and uncertain, and then promptly work to regress back to stage three or even two at times. I think this might be normal. Few of us follow a straight line in our spiritual story: we squiggle and wiggle, stop and start, progress and regress, rest and recoup, charge ahead recklessly and take sharp turns or stumble into ditches that turn out to be portals. This isn't a bad thing. On the contrary, I think it's the thing that makes your story special and beautiful. "There are years that ask questions and years that answer,"[7] wrote Zora Neale Hurston. The writer of Ecclesiastes would agree: there is a season for everything.

I think this is why we can learn to hold both the answers and the questions lightly, alongside the joy and the grief, the education and the experience. The Holy Spirit breathes in the years that ask questions and our years that answer them. Some answers are simply lived into, stumbled into, born into, slept into, wept into. And *Some answers are simply lived into, stumbled into, born into, slept into, wept into.* in the midst of this all, I have found that, as Peter and John preached to the religious leaders in that story I told you earlier, Christ is the cornerstone of it all.

Where else could I go, Lord? You have the words of eternal life.[8]

We live out of our imperfect answers. We want so much to do things right, that it seems odd to start even before we're ready. We want our ducks in a row, our answers indexed in three-ring binders. But instead, this is faith at its core.

We're not always ready. We don't always have the answers to our questions. But everyone gets to play. Often the first answer I have for my question begins with "Wherever you go, I'll follow."

4

Getting into the Word

ON READING THE BIBLE

Redemption shows up in odd places. I grew up primarily in the Word of Faith movement, a fringe of the charismatic-Pentecostal renewals that places a strong emphasis on lining up our words and our thoughts with our readings of Scripture. We believed that physical, emotional, spiritual, and financial healing would be found through "speaking the Word," which to us, meant certain verses were to be spoken out loud because faith comes by hearing, and hearing by the Word of God. We believed that the power of our words brought us into agreement with God and that the best words to speak were, of course, the words of Scripture. I can critique this movement with the best of them, but one thing for which I remain grateful is the way that Scripture worked its way into my imagination and my soul. Those words gave me a picture of a God who was joyous and who longed for relationship, healing, and wholeness for us all. Scripture has been God's primary way of breaking through my boxes and presuppositions; it surprises me, challenges me, and changes me.

But I had to learn that taking the Bible seriously doesn't

mean taking everything literally. I had to learn to read the whole Bible through the lens of Jesus, and I had to learn to stop making it into something it wasn't—a glorified answer book or rule book or magic spell. I had to stop trying to reduce the Bible to something I could tame or wield as a tool. I had to let the Bible be everything it was meant to be, to cast away the idols of certainty, materialism, and control.

* * *

I used to call the Bible "the Word." I try not to do that anymore.

I would read the opening chapter of the Gospel of John and think it was talking about the Bible: "The Word was first, the Word present to God, God present to the Word. The Word was God, in readiness for God from day one" (John 1:1–2 NLT). I'd characterize my time reading the Bible as "time in the Word." Capital W. When I had a problem, my first solution was "I need to get the Word on that"—our cultural shorthand for saying that surely there was a Bible verse to cure whatever was ailing.

If I had kept reading that chapter of the Bible in context instead of cherry-picking, I would have seen it sooner perhaps: the Word is actually Jesus. John was writing about Jesus, not about a Bible that didn't even exist yet. It was Jesus—the Word of God—who "became flesh and blood, and moved into the neighborhood" (John 1:14 MSG). In fact, the end of that exactly poetic and beautiful telling of the story of Jesus ends by showing us the way to understand the rest of Scripture in light of Jesus: "We got the basics from Moses, and then this exuberant giving and receiving, this endless knowing and understanding—all this came through Jesus, the Messiah. No one has ever seen God, not so much as a glimpse. This one-of-a-kind God-Expression, who exists at the very heart of the Father, has made Him plain as day."[1]

I think I used to elevate the Bible to being a fourth member of the Trinity. I yearned for systematic theology with charts and graphs and easy-to-decode secrets. I wanted answers and clarity—the cry of the modern reader. But the more I read of the Bible, the more confused I became. So much of the Bible didn't line up with what I had been taught about the Bible. Old Testament scholar Peter Enns summed me right up when he said that the problem isn't the Bible, "the problem is coming to the Bible with expectations it's not set up to bear."[2]

The Bible wasn't meant to fulfill those expectations any more than it was meant to receive my worship.

My expectation was divinity, simplicity, infallibility, literalism, easy answers.

The Bible wasn't meant to fulfill those expectations any more than it was meant to receive my worship.

* * *

Pause with me for a moment. We've been working hard at our little rummage sale. Have I mentioned yet how avoidance is part of our sorting? It's true. We see these questions or doubts or wonderings out of the corner of our eyes, and we think that if we ignore them, they will go away. Or we simply know that we aren't ready for that one just yet. It feels too big to manage, too scary, too sacred. We've all seen it in our lives. The room we can't enter because we know the contents are too much for our fragile emotions. The box of letters we can't bring ourselves to read yet. The basements of our grandfathers remain untouched because we are still grieving or afraid or simply too busy with life. Urgency isn't always with us at the sort, and so we learn to sit with the mess until the time is right for the organizing or examining, for the storytelling and the claiming.

Sometimes we avoid sorting because it's painful. It brings up bad memories, perhaps. And I think we're totally fine to let some things sit for a while. I know that for me that process of sorting through my faith is an ongoing one. Just when I think I've settled things, I spot another corner that needs a second look. Or I revisit something that I thought was settled and realize, "Oh, no wait, I actually don't need this anymore, I can let it go, it's just clutter."

> *Just when I think I've settled things, I spot another corner that needs a second look.*

I think that this is part of the process.

And when we examine the deeper issues of our beliefs or questions—particularly when the roots of those beliefs are not merely information but gut-level experience rooted in sadness and grief—well, it is sacred ground or scary ground, a minefield. That's okay.

One thing I've learned is that the Holy Spirit can be trusted. When the time is right, the time is right.

* * *

Maybe we're asking the wrong questions about the Bible. Peter Enns says, "This is the Bible we have, the Bible where God meets us. Not a book kept at safe distance from the human drama. Not a fragile Bible that has to be handled with care lest it crumble in our hands. Not a book that has to be defended 24/7 to make sure our faith doesn't dissolve. In other words, not an artificially well-behaved Bible that gives false comfort, but the Holy Bible, the Word of God, with wrinkles, complexities, unexpected maneuvers, and downright strangeness. This is the Bible God has given His people. This Bible is worth reading and paying attention to, because this is the Bible God uses, as He always has, to point His readers to deeper trust in Him. We are free to walk away from this invitation, of course, but we are not free to make the Bible in our own image. What the Bible looks like is God's call, not ours." [3]

I think it's both hard work and good work to challenge our own assumptions. How unfortunate to use the Bible as a conversation stopper, not a starting point. And yet the Bible is not simply "the text" either—on par with every other book. It's a sacramental reading, a holy reading. But

"We are free to walk away from this invitation, of course, but we are not free to make the Bible in our own image."

this means loving the reality of the Bible, instead of the ideal of a modern construct.

The book we've been given is for a purpose as it is. N. T. Wright lectured that "the Bible, then, is designed to function through human beings, through the Church, through people who, living still by the Spirit, have their life molded by this Spirit-inspired book. What for? Well, as Jesus said in John 20, 'As the Father sent me, even so I send you.' He sends the Church into the world, in other words, to be and do for the world what He was and did for Israel." [4]

The purpose of the Bible is to equip us to be sent out into the world, to proclaim the Kingdom of God, to lift up our eyes and see each other and see God at work—and then, to participate fully in that life. Now.

And let's be honest: being a Christian is sometimes almost at odds with what we read in some parts of Scripture. We can

be entirely "biblical" and yet be far from being a disciple of
Jesus Christ.

* * *

In our early years of parenting, Brian and I began to read a
children's Bible storybook aloud. I was trying to be a good

*We can be entirely
"biblical" and yet be far
from being a disciple of
Jesus Christ.*

mother, and wasn't reading Bible
stories part of being a good mother?
That was when I began skipping
big sections of Scripture. I wasn't
able to turn off my pathos. Noah
and the Ark? All I could see in my
mind were animals and people drowning in terror. Jericho?
Forget your fun Sunday school songs, this was genocide. The
story of Hannah, giving up her son Samuel to temple, broke
my new-mother heart. I faltered before a God who would ask
such a thing of a mother. I read the story of David and Bathsheba as an adult, and suddenly I saw Bathsheba as a victim,
possibly of rape but at the very least, a victim of patriarchy,
an unequal power structure that left her without choice. Story
after story in the Bible disturbed me, and so I would skip and
skip and skip as I tried to read the Bible to help my children
form an idea of God. Because what sort of God would tell His
people to dash the brains of babies against the rocks? What
sort of God would ask Abraham to sacrifice his son as a "test"
of obedience?

One day, while I was reading a story from the Old Testament
to my child, she asked me, "Is God the bad guy in this one? Or
the good guy?"

Sometimes I felt like I was asking that same question.

* * *

When I was a kid, I wondered if God got born again between the Old and New Testament. Maybe that was the reason God seemed to "change" from the ancient stories to the Jesus I knew and loved, to the God of love spoken of so fervently by John, the God who was bridegroom to a yearning bride, the one who had only to say "follow me" for people to drop everything and run after. But no, we still have people who perceive God as the ancients perceived Him—as vindictive or petty or warmongering, filled with hate. It's not that God got born again between Malachi and Matthew; it's that God became incarnate among us and revealed the truth: God is Love.

But now that I realize that Jesus was the Word, the rest of the Bible could be seen through the Cross. Besides, the whole story of God isn't exclusively in the Bible. After all, the Old Testament is the story of the nation of Israel in particular. A basic level of anthropology will tell us that many ancient cultures have similar stories—the Flood, for instance. Who can limit God to one book or one culture? I imagine God moving among all cultures and all nations in unique and beautiful ways right from the dawn of time. I love the stories from colonial missionaries who arrived in distant lands to convert unreached people groups, only to discover that they had already encountered Jesus on their own. Dreams, visions, divine encounters, all testifying to Jesus Christ.

The Bible is subordinate to Jesus, and the Spirit reveals the letters, all while we use the Scriptures to interpret and understand other verses of the Bible. We read with the hermeneutic of Jesus intact: How did Jesus explain the Scriptures, teach us to live? Does this interpretation move us further into under-standing the nature and character of God, toward compassion, love, justice, reconciliation, and above all, resurrection and redemption? After all, God didn't physically write the Bible; this treasure was inspired by the Spirit, but it's a treasure in earthen vessels.[5]

Much of the Bible is the story of our fallible people seeking to understand and follow God. For instance, regarding the story of Israel's war with the Canaanites—when Israel not only van-quished the enemies but went on to kill every man, woman, and child—Peter Enns argues that God never told the Israelites to kill the Canaanites. The Israelites *believed* that God told them to kill the Canaanites.[6] This way of reading Scripture made more sense to me. It was more in line with Jesus, more in line with the way He taught us how we had misunderstood and mis-represented God even in our histories.

After all, the Israelites saw God in tribal ways. How else would they experience God but within their unique place and time?

"The Bible is the story of God told from the limited point of view of real people living at a certain place and time. The Bible looks the way it does because 'God lets His children tell the story,' so to speak," writes Enns. These ancient writers had an adequate understanding of God for them in their time, but not for all of time, and if we take that to heart, we will actually be in a better position to respect these ancient voices and see what they have to say rather than whitewashing the details and making up "explanations" to ease our stress. For Christians, the Gospel has always been the lens through which Israel's stories are read—which means, for Christians, Jesus, not the

Bible, has the final word. "Jesus was bigger than the Bible," argues Enns.[7]

* * *

There are other examples of God's redemptive movement in Scripture, ways that God has worked within human history to move the arc of justice further into His divine plan, to draw us into life in the Kingdom of God. And the funny thing is that Jesus often performed these acts of redemptive movement without a lot of justification for the religious elite. He simply taught and lived into the eternal reality. But I imagine that if you were a religious elite at the time, the movement—and how Jesus embarked upon it in the midst of a real walking-around life— was more infuriating than funny. After all, Jesus would say, "You have heard it said . . . but I say . . . ," and then suddenly everything gets flipped into a newness of life and spirit, superseding the rules, fulfilling the law by transcending it, even. When Jesus first taught, "You have heard that it was said, "Eye for eye and tooth for tooth," but I tell you . . . love your enemies and pray for those who persecute you,"[8] it was electrifying. It still is. After all, we still prefer an eye for an eye. Love your enemies? Honestly, that Jesus can be so unrealistic.

Another story that comes to mind concerns keeping the Sabbath holy. In Numbers 15:32–36, a man is discovered to be gathering sticks on the Sabbath. The Israelites apprehend him but don't quite know what to do next. The text says that Moses then heard from the Lord: the man must be killed for his sin. And so they stoned the man to death.

A truly gruesome tale, I don't mind saying from my perch in early twenty-first-century Canada.

But then in the New Testament, Jesus heals a man on—wait for it—the Sabbath. In John 5:1–16, Jesus returns to Jerusalem and visits the pool of Bethesda, where He encounters a man who had been sick for thirty-eight years. Jesus says with authority, "Stand up, pick up your mat, and walk!" and the man is healed. The Jewish leaders object—of course, they do. They had been taught by Moses that all work on the Sabbath was wrong, even good work. But Jesus replies to the leaders, "My Father is always working, and so am I." Not only did He break the Sabbath, but now He had dared to call God His father. And He said His father is *always* working—apparently, even on the Sabbath. And so we return to John 1, the Scripture that started this chapter and started my journey to rereading the Bible through the lens of Jesus. In verse 17, "For the law was given through Moses, but God's unfailing love and faithfulness came through Jesus Christ."

Jesus reveals God, the true God. And we know that God doesn't change; Jesus is the same—yesterday, today, and forever. The law was given through Moses, but God's unfailing love and faithfulness came through Jesus Christ. In John 14:8–9, Philip said, "Lord, show us the Father and that will be enough for us." Jesus answered: "Don't you know me, Philip, even after I have been among you such a long time? Anyone who has seen me has seen the Father. How can you say, 'Show us the Father'?"

At times in my life, I have had the wrong view of God. I imagine some of what I think about God right now is laughable, if not outright wrong. It's okay. A lot of us are wrong about God—including people in the Bible.

Much of Scripture relates our perception or understanding of God. The God who called us His friends, His beloved children, the God who characterized Godself as "Abba"—the tender Hebrew word for *Daddy*—is also the God of the Old Testament. So anytime Deity is inconsistent with Jesus, it must be that we don't know what we don't know because we don't yet know Jesus.

God isn't a different God than He was in the Old Testament; it's just that Jesus gave us a new perspective, the true perspective, on God. And in stark relief, the Bible shows us this very truth.

Jesus came to show us the true God: God in the world and in our lives and in our relationships with one another. If we want to know what God is like, we can look to Jesus. And if we want to read the Bible well, we need to start with Jesus and remain in Jesus, and we need to let Jesus explain it. The Bible doesn't trump Jesus; Jesus interprets the Bible.

In that same chapter of John when Jesus heals the man on the Sabbath, He rebukes the religious leaders: "You search the Scriptures because you think they give you eternal life. But the Scriptures point to me! Yet you refuse to come to me to receive this life."[9]

As Brian Zahnd writes, "The supreme value of the treasure that is Holy Scripture is that it is the divine witness to the Word of God who is Christ."[10]

* * *

The story and the song of Scripture have haunted me. Once I stepped outside my selective reading of pet Scripture verses, I discovered that the Bible was so much more—poetry, history, narrative, law, wisdom, prophecy, encouragement, personal letters, a love story of the ways that we have perceived God and the ways God has broken through those perceptions to substantive life.

I had to sit with the story that haunted me, to wrestle with it well. As my friend Rachel says, "If you aren't questioning the Bible, I have to wonder if you're even reading it."

For instance, I never liked the Apostle Paul very much. (Apparently you can type a sentence like that and not be struck by lightning.)

Like many Christians, I am still drawn toward certain personalities within the Bible. My heart has always aligned itself with the Apostle John: so many aspects of his character and story and passions oddly sing to me. I feel that I understand him, or perhaps, that he would understand me. My sister has always had a soft spot for Peter. Perhaps you identify more with Deborah or David, Elizabeth or Joseph. Sometimes it's because we see our own priorities and passions and stories represented in them.

But Paul?

I have had Some Big Thoughts and Feelings about the Apostle Paul.

He wrote a lot of the Scripture that is often used against women's full equality within the Church. Well-meaning people have used Paul's writings to justify abuse or silencing, oppression and marginalization against women, so, yes, of course I would have an issue with Paul. To me, he was a misogynist. He was narrow-minded and bossy. He was snippy. As a feminist, I was suspicious of Paul. I even avoided his words in Scripture. Instead, I camped out in the Gospels, in John's epistles, in Hebrews, in the Psalms and Proverbs. My friend Kelley taught me how to

Well-meaning people have used Paul's writings against women to justify abuse or silencing, so, yes, of course I would have an issue with Paul.

love Exodus and Isaiah and the Old Testament prophets, helping me to understand the liberation story of Scripture, a few
years ago, and this changed my life. As I grew in the faith, of
course I began to read the whole canon of Scripture, but when
it came to Paul's writings, I almost had to forget that Paul had
written them. It was easier to receive the words if I forgot that
Paul was the one who dictated or scribed them. That might
sound strange to you at first reading, but for people who have
had the Bible used against them as a weapon, it makes terrible
sense.

An abusive or oppressive reading of Scripture has consequences. I have friends who are unable to read Scripture in
the translations of their childhood—the King James version,
for instance—because they still bear scars on their hearts
and bodies from the way the Bible was used against them. We
can respect each other's struggles with Scripture because they
are often born out of our pain. It can be difficult to call God
"Father" when the only father you've known is disappointment
or abuse or absence. But God transcends our labels and our
translations to meet us right where we are, right in the midst of
our story, in the midst of our pain, in the midst of our trauma.

So I think it's entirely appropriate if the only way we can feel
safe in God is to take a break from reading the Bible entirely
or to read it with new words or eyes or voices. Until we can
untangle the lie, it's hard to receive the beauty and truth. The
Spirit isn't limited to meeting us only in the words of the Bible.
And when the time is right to return to Scripture, to be able to
fully embrace and love the gift of it, then the time will be right.
That's one of the reasons I often use the Message paraphrase
of Scripture when I'm teaching or writing—it doesn't have as
much baggage for the wounded among us. The words aren't as

familiar, and so we can often receive what the Spirit wants to speak; we can rest in new words because the old ones are too heavy to bear any longer.

As I was writing my first book, *Jesus Feminist*, a strange transformation took place in me: I began to love Paul. Really, truly love him as a brother, precisely *because* I was writing about life on the other side of the gender debates, advocating for the full equality of women.

It started with those clobber verses—anyone who has been on the receiving end, you know the ones—2 Timothy, Titus 2, Ephesians 5, and so on. I did my research long before the day came to write, but as a refresher, I dug out the commentaries and books again. Responsible author, I wanted to make sure I had my hermeneutical ducks in a row.

But as I worked my way through the passages of Scripture that I used to hate, I began to see Paul more clearly, to understand Scripture even better. I began to see his wisdom, his subversion, his heart. When I looked at his full ministry—how he praised and esteemed women in leadership in the Church, how he turned household codes within a patriarchal society on their heads, how he used feminine metaphors, how he subverted the systems, how he passionately defended equality—the verses that used to clobber me began to embrace me.

The truth broke through. I wasn't fighting *against* Paul—I was fighting *with* him. I read Paul's words in Scripture and I began to realize I had not known him, his world, his context, his brilliance. I had been silenced or shut down by people putting words in his mouth or intent in his words that he never intended. I had missed so much of the beauty of Paul.

By reading Paul without any thought for context or place,

narrative or history, I had nearly missed a great gift. We miss the Gospel forest for the word-by-word trees; we miss the Story by picking and choosing. The whole of Paul's teaching and beliefs about women in the Church or in society could not be con-

We miss the Gospel forest for the word-by-word trees.

tained in a few lines from an ancient letter. Not when we consider the truth that women were leading, ministering, praying, prophesying, teaching, managing, and financing throughout the Church—with Paul's full knowledge and blessing.

For instance, in 1 Corinthians 14:39, Paul encouraged women to prophesy alongside of their brothers, just as Peter spoke the words of the prophet Joel at the time of Pentecost: "In that day, I will pour out my Spirit, your sons and your daughters all prophesy." I began to see that what the scholars taught me was true: Paul subverted the Greco-Roman household codes to ensure the safety and honor of the most vulnerable in society— women, children, and slaves. He worked within a patriarchal society that he was convinced would soon be over because of the coming return of Jesus. And it turned out that most of those "women be silent" lines were about specific problems in specific churches—at times, even having to do with one particular, singular woman, not all womankind forever and ever amen.

Among the early church leaders, Paul was consistently a voice for freedom and equality, for welcoming the ones considered outsiders or misfits or unclean or unworthy. One of his great passions was the freedom we have found in Christ and the truth that we all belong, no matter what. As he wrote so beautifully in his letter to the Galatians, "You are all children of God through faith in Christ Jesus. And all who have been united with Christ in baptism have put on Christ, like putting on new clothes. There is no longer Jew or Gentile, slave or free, male and female. For you are all one in Christ Jesus."[11]

Page after page, word by word, the theology of freedom settled back into my bones, just as Paul would have celebrated.

Now I think that if Paul knew how a few of his words had been twisted, misinterpreted, and misapplied against women, he would be brokenhearted.

Oddly, I even began to love Paul for the very imperfect humanness of him in the words of the text: his frustrations, his love, his exhaustion, his habit of confronting his elders or leaders boldly, his stubbornness, his jealousy, his passion, his intelligence, his impatience, his impeccable sarcasm, his snark. All of it. Instead of seeing him as infallible or unmovable, I became thankful for his unedited self as seen in the Scriptures, the ways that he seemed to change and grow before my eyes. He gave me permission to remember that he was a man, that he was not Jesus, that he didn't have a more direct line to the Spirit, that we all have moments of impatience and vulnerability, that he was just like the rest of us.

He wasn't perfect. He was complex, yes, but oh, such diamond-like, multifaceted brilliance. Poet theologian, evangelist and pastor, leader and thorn in the side. A radical, contradictory truth-teller, a teacher with a tender father heart, a broken and humble servant—all Paul.

His crazy beautiful words about freedom with responsibility, about mutual submission, about trusting in Christ and not the law, about loving one another, about our Jesus . . . He is my brother, indeed. His story changed me. I loved Jesus better because I began to understand how and why Paul loved Him too. As these realizations settled in my heart, I began to ask, *What else have I been missing?*

What I thought I knew or what I thought I believed turned out to be seeing through a glass darkly. Even now, I am fairly certain I only have a small candle to aid my vision.

What else had I missed? What other ways had I mischaracterized truth or misunderstood the Bible?

* * *

There is no end to the ways God will work in and through the Scriptures to reach us. We read the Bible as it reads us;[12] it is the two-edged sword rightly dividing truth, separating and seeing through us. How we read and study Scripture—and then how that reading changes minds and hearts and lives—is a great testimony of the Spirit's activity in us and through us.

> *We read the Bible as it reads us.*

I now have a higher view of Scripture than ever before. As Brian McLaren wrote, "The Bible is too good and too important to be left to those who won't think critically about it. And frankly, it is too dangerous."[13]

* * *

In the mornings when I woke up, my father was already awake. He would get ready for work and then sit down with his coffee to read the Bible. He sought out the promises of God and wrote them next to our names. When my exams were looming, he would write longhand beside my name the words of James 1:5: "If you need wisdom, ask our generous God, and He will give it to you. He will not rebuke you for asking."

Did James speak that word specifically for me? For me in the early nineties, as I went through high school in Canada? Nope. But the heart of the God that Scripture reveals is the same for us all, and so we asked for wisdom as I studied chemistry, my great nemesis, and we believed God would not rebuke us for asking. James taught us to pray this way.

When I graduated from university, we had a small family party and my parents presented me with a cake. The icing bore the words of Jeremiah 29:11, "For I know the plans I have for you, declares the Lord, plans to prosper you and not to harm you, plans to give you a hope and a future." Years before, they told me that they had prayed and that God had led them to that verse as a guide for my life ahead. They called it my "life verse." By "life verse," they were saying that it was meant to be a blessing to me and an anchor, to speak life over me and to help me. It was meant to be something I turn to, something I memorize so that the words would always be hidden in my heart whenever I needed encouragement and focus, a mighty rock to cling to in times of rough water.

It's such a cliché now—the graduate with the Jeremiah 29:11 life verse. There are vast swaths of Christian junk imprinted with that reference. But it wasn't cliché to me in that moment, because I believed. And of course, I now know that we were entirely taking it out of context: Jeremiah was writing to a whole group of people, not to an individual, and he was writing to the ones who had been taken captive to Babylon, promising redemption after seventy years in exile. You can read it yourself, in the verse just before. This wasn't meant for me; it wasn't meant for my context. It's much more life-and-death than what I was experiencing at the time.

Yet I filled my heart with the words and took them personally. And I think there's room for that in the story of Scripture too. We can respect the context and the purpose. We can avoid the temptation to make ourselves the main character in the story of Scripture. We can know that this verse is specific to a time and a place and a people. And at the same time, we can write down Bible verses on index cards and tape them to our mirrors, believing in the heart of the God for whom these words prophesy. The Spirit can breathe through the most mundane moments of our lives; why wouldn't she breathe through the words of Scripture for me too? Why would we restrict in such a way? Why wouldn't we embrace the God these words reveal?

I've found over the years since then that it has indeed been my "life verse" in ways my parents couldn't have foreseen. When I struggled with direction in my life, when I lost my babies, when I was confused, angry, lost, or afraid, this verse would rise up out of the ashes of my heart and remind me that God had plans for me, good plans, and that I have hope. It amazes me how many times in my life I have turned to these thirty simple words for comfort.

So our tinies each have a life verse. My return to this practice was even more dear to me because of my wrestling with Scripture and what it means and what it's for—in the world and in my life. In the evenings while I was pregnant, I would pore through the Bible, praying, and wait. Wait for that quickening in my spirit when I was reading, that jump in my heart as if to say, *Ah, yes. This is it.* As if the Spirit were spotlighting the words, I always knew when I found the right verse. It just fit.

Then we would pray these verses over our babies. I would whisper them into their baby hair when we rocked in the middle of the night. I wrote their verses in their baby books. We put the words up on the walls in their rooms. We chose verses that contain our hopes, prayers, and dreams for their lives. We're a bit out of context, a bit simple. We pray, hiding the Word in their hearts—and our own. We pray that we're setting them on a good path, so that when they are old, they will not depart from it.

And yes, one of the tinies was given Jeremiah 29:11 as a life verse.

* * *

This is my morning now: I chase everyone out the door in the morning to their designated destinations. Brian to work, the older two tinies to the school bus. I put the baby down for a nap. Our preschooler watches cartoons for a bit while I have my cuppa tea and my peanut butter toast—at last. (I always wait to eat breakfast until it's a bit more peaceful in the house. I hate to feel like I'm bolting my food down in a race.) And then I open my Bible, just like my father did every morning of his life. I know that this very morning, he was also in what he still calls "the Word." And I am my father's daughter. I am in the Word, just not quite in the same way anymore. I spend these moments reading Isaiah and I pray. I write and I refill my cup, I bow my head over these sacred words that I love all the better for the wrestling to release them from the prison I built for them.

I bow my head over these sacred words that I love all the better for the wrestling to release them from the prison I built for them.

I begin to read, jotting down verses as the Spirit illuminates them to me. I can't always explain how this works, but as I read the Bible, it sometimes feels as if certain passages or words take on a brightness to my eyes, an illumination, and I think, *I need to write this down.*

Writing things down is my way of remembering them. In my memory, I don't remember phrases, I remember the sight of my own handwriting and the words that I wrote down so carefully.

Sometimes I write the names of my four tinies and then I write down a few words from Scripture that correspond with what I am praying over them. For the one who has struggled with feeling rested, I write that God has promised His beloved sweet sleep (Psalm 127:2), that my loved one's body and soul will rest and confidently dwell in safety (Proverbs 3:24). For the one who is struggling with oversensitivity, I write down the words of Ephesians 6:10, praying for strength in the Lord and in His mighty power.

I haven't purposely memorized a lot of Scripture, but it's through me and in me anyways, because it's often the language of my prayers. I come boldly, barefaced, to the presence of God.

Scripture shapes my prayers, the words and images, the metaphors and poems, the declarations and promises. And I keep praying because it's my first language, the language of my spirit, my connection with Love.

If we want to know what God is really, truly like, we look to Christ first: the Scriptures testify to Jesus, not the other way around.

So here I am, my father's daughter, as the light breaks through the forest, writing down the names of my children and my husband, my friends and even the world at large—like our brothers and sisters in Iraq or Haiti or Burundi—and beside these scrawled names, I am writing out the words of Scripture. Not like promises or talismans, not like magic spells, no. But to give language to what I yearn for, what I believe, and even what I hope. It's my way of walking in the counsel of the Holy Spirit, may our hearts be fixed and established on Jesus.

I cling more to my Bible now than I used to; I lean more heavily on the stories and the promises, on the visions and the hope. I am challenged and changed in ways I never was when I took every word literally—now that I take them so seriously. Now the Bible places a demand on both my mind and my heart; now I finish with my hands open and prayer in my throat, a fire in my bones and worship rising up, and the ferocious appetite to be transformed, even more, into the likeness of Jesus, into the heart God has for humanity.

The People of God

ON CHURCH

I stand in the front row of the church—a few dozen of us in a community center—clapping along to the repetitive and simple praise choruses about the exodus of Israel and the blood of Jesus with repeated proclamations of *hosanna. The horse and the rider are thrown into the sea!* Three tambourines in a small room make quite a racket. The ladies wave banners, the children dance. I am overly earnest even for a kid. I throw my skinny child arms into the sky and sing loudly: *As the deer panteth for the water, so my soul longeth after you.*

Later: I am standing in a gigantic stadium, thousands of people around me. The music is loud, the performance dazzling. *Church shouldn't be boring!* we declare. We sing songs of the victorious, the conquering. I feel like crying, feel like jumping, like running. I feel alive, every cell thrumming with passion. Look at us, so young and beautiful and blind, testifying to love in three-part harmony. We are self-declared world changers. The devil better watch out.

Later: The liturgy of the charismatic evangelicals is empty to me. Dead religion perhaps. Every prayer begins with *Father, we just . . .* And I find myself admitting, *Father, I just can't hear you here anymore. Maybe I never did.*

Later: The preacher stands up on the stage in his designer suit and declares "Money cometh!" to a congregation of poor students. The seeds of skepticism and disillusion I carefully keep hidden grow long tendrils around my faith. I am sick to death of prosperity teaching masking the poverty of the soul and of ignoring the cries for justice from the oppressed. I am sick of vending machine prayers, performance, easy answers, and formulas that don't add up. I am sick of feeling like a misbehaving cog in someone else's broken-down machine. I get up. I walk up the aisle to the exit, my hands push against the heavy wooden doors, and I walk right out of church as an act of protest for the first time.

Later: I am standing in my yard in Texas, smoking cigarettes and praying in tongues. By now, I am married to a boy turned pastor, and yet every Sunday I want to skip church because I do not feel there is room there for my grief.

Later: Brian and I are in a red Chevy, headed north. After trying my best to be a Good Christian Woman, I have cashed in my credentials. I quit church, done with performances, done with ministry. Angry and exhausted, I am spilling over with opinions on all the ways that "they" were wrong. Every passing kilometer shakes a layer of homesickness off my soul. No one is counting on me for the answers—the freedom of it. By the time we hit Washington State, the pine trees reappear and then, an unexpected spark of hope. *This is not the end of my story.* My hands grip the steering wheel, and I press a bit harder on the gas.

Later: I am heavily pregnant and kneeling at the altar rail in the cathedral. When I couldn't find my way back to Jesus through the clutter of praise and worship and church as I knew it, I find God in the silence. I lift my hands to light a candle and I bow my head. The only sound is the faint noise of traffic from the urban rush-and-go just outside the narthex. I am alone in an unlocked stone church. I find myself humming without thinking, *As the deer panteth for the water, so my soul longeth after thee.* I haven't said those words in decades. But I raise my hands up in the air, and the baby we have so desired kicks and I cry and cry and cry with relief and longing. *Oh, here you are. I thought I'd lost you. I thought I'd never feel this again.*

Later: I am working in an office just down the hall from the multipurpose room filled with the bravest women I know in my real life. I listen to these beautiful women sing about being redeemed. I know their stories; each one of them still has a long road ahead. I place my forehead down onto the cool white Ikea desk and breathe in their faith. Jesus has become real to me, and so I can't pretend anymore that I am not just as much of a mess as everyone else. In fact, the freedom I am finding is exactly that: I am learning alongside the girls of the residential home that I'm a mess and I'm beloved, both together, and this is not the end.

Later: I am standing under a canvas roof in the tent city of Port-au-Prince after the earthquake. *Then sings my soul,* we cry out, *my Savior God to thee, how great thou art, how great thou art.* There is a little girl in a blue gingham dress trimmed in printed strawberries and she is singing. She was sweeping a dirt floor just a few moments ago. I am out of place but my hands are open and I am singing anyway.

Later: I am holding another small, sleepy child, my greatest ministry so far. We rock slowly in the midnight hours. We are silent together, one small head pressed up against my breast, listening to my heart beat. I have wrapped us in a quilt, the rocker creaks, and a small hoarse voice says, "Mumma, you sing?" I begin to whisper-sing into the darkness: *As the deer panteth for the water, so my soul longeth after thee. You alone are my heart's desire and I long to worship thee.* When he finally sleeps, I lay him in his bed and return to the living room. I light a candle in the darkness, for the silence, for the other souls who are still awake with their babies. Minutes later, I blow it out and go to bed.

Later: I catch sight of an old woman sitting in the front row of church on Sunday. She sits beside her husband of nearly sixty years—in her best Sunday clothes among a congregation of blue jeans—her wrinkled hands barely raised into the air. No one behind her would know her hands are up, but I can see her singing quietly, every single word on her lips, tears rolling down her face, her hands are unclenched, her palms wide open.

* * *

I feel tenderhearted now, when I look back at my own self in those seasons. And I feel tenderhearted toward all the people who were there with me, all of us doing the best we could with what we had.

I am reclaiming Church.

In God, we live and move and have our being. Now I know that God was in and among the movements of my life and that He was moving in the people around me too. I now see outside and in and among, and above all, for us, for us all.

I am learning to gather up all these disparate seasons and thoughts and opinions and experiences, to hold them in my hands with gratitude.

Now I'm able to find something good in them all: in the

over-the-top excessive prosperity preachers and the smug theologians and the pot-stirring elitists and the overly passionate kids in the stadium light shows and the disillusioned, bitter cynics. Because here is the truth: I'm all of those things too. Someday I'll add the woman I am now, the theology I practice, the words I write so earnestly to that list. I know I will.

There's room for all of us. There's room for all of me.

Maybe I believe this because I'm gratefully disillusioned about church leadership. Maybe it's because I'm pretty convinced that we're all doing the best we can do, most of the time. Maybe it's because I don't think anyone has the corner on truth. Maybe it's because I'm thankful for the extremes and all points in between, because they keep us growing, keep us alive, keep us reforming. Maybe it's because I've been wrong so often. Maybe it's because I'm a bit tired. And maybe I want a little more kindness.

I suppose it's possible that someday the Church will look at me with disdain on their faces and mock Twitter accounts from coffee shops and write doctoral dissertations on all the ways I did it wrong, and all I'll know how to say is that I know and I'm sorry and I hope I learned to be kind.

* * *

My husband tends to be more of an idealist than me, meaning that he likes to make our decisions based on our ideals. I prefer to make decisions based on the reality before us, what is *actually* going on instead of what *should be* going on. After we left full-time vocational ministry, Brian wanted to talk about what church could be, ought to be, should be, would be, was meant to be. He wanted to go to church to *be* the Church the way that we understood it. And sure, the ideals sounded beautiful, but I was too caught up in the reality of my lifelong experiences with church and the way it functioned to buy into the ideals alone. My experiences in church ranged widely over the years. But when my husband left ministry and we were both limping home to Canada—burned out, burned up, exhausted—one thing was sure: the reality was pretty far from the ideal.

So even though Brian still refused to give up on the Church as an ideal, in reality I opted to stop going to church. For six years.

* * *

When my parents became Christians during my childhood, every Sunday of my life was spent in some sort of worship gathering. Even in the dead of winter in Winnipeg, when every vehicle required a minimum of twenty minutes idling to "warm up" as well as a vigorous windshield scraping, we went to church. Stomping snow off our boots in the foyer, we hung up our parkas, took off our boots, and put on our church shoes. My dad would say that he looked forward to church all week; it was the only time we got to be with other believers. "Oh, it's so good to be in the house of the Lord!" he'd say even if we were just meeting with a couple of other families in somebody's basement or a drafty school gym. I understood why my mother loved church: she was gregarious and outgoing, so of course she liked church. But for my dad to need and love church? Well, that was a different matter: my father is an introvert like me. Our shared idea of hell is endless small talk in large crowds of people. But he did love going to church—not because it was perfect, but because it mattered.

I spent my high school years going to church Sunday mornings, then prowling downtown Calgary in the afternoons with the rest of the youth group, looking for movies that cost only a loonie. Then we'd head back to church for an evening service. I spent Wednesday and Friday nights at youth events, whole weeks of my summer at church camp. In university, I went to chapel services twice a week, and I woke up early on Sundays to catch the shuttle bus for worship in one-after-another mega-churches around Tulsa. As a resident adviser, I'd come back to the dorms to perform "church check"—knocking on doors to see who was still sleeping versus who was a good Christian. The girls on my floor could have been at Taco Cabana for all I knew; as long as they weren't in bed, they got credit for church.

Then my husband became a pastor, and we were at church all the time, consumed by church; everything in our life rose and set on church. It was exhausting. Go to church, go to church, church church church church. My friends were from church, the guy we bought our house from went to our church, the lady who cut our hair went to our church, our neighbors all went to our church.

Perhaps the next six years of church avoidance were simply a rather logical overcorrection.

* * *

Here is what I wish someone would have told me at the beginning of those six years:

Perhaps we never can really leave our mother church. The complexity of tangled up roots isn't easily undone. And yes, I think there is a way to reclaim and redeem our traditions with an eye on the future.

But maybe this isn't your time to do that. Maybe this is your time to let go and walk away. You'll be surprised where you end up.

If you have needed to walk away, I know you're grieving. Let yourself grieve. When something ends, it's worthwhile to notice its passing, to sit in the space and look at the pieces before you head out.

In the early days, when you first walk away, you may feel afraid. You don't need to be afraid. It can be confusing to separate from what so-and-so-big-guy-in-the-big-organization says about you or people like you. It can be disorienting to walk out into the wilderness on purpose. It can be lonely. It can be exhilarating. It can be terrifying.

My friend, don't stay in a religious institution or a religious tradition out of fear. Fear should not drive your decisions: let love motivate you.

Lean into your questions and your doubts until you find that God is out here in the wilderness too.[1]

Lean into your questions and your doubts until you find that God is out here in the wilderness too.

I have good news for you, brokenhearted one: God is here in the wandering. In fact, you might just find, as Jonathan Martin wrote, that the wilderness is the birthplace of true intimacy with God.

Jesus isn't only in your tradition. You get to love Jesus without being an evangelical or a Pentecostal or a Presbyterian or whatever new label you've acquired these days or old label that just doesn't fit anymore.

Your pet gatekeeper isn't the sole arbitrator of the Christian faith: there is more complexity and beauty and diversity of voices and experiences within followers of the Way than you know. Remember, your view of Christians, your personal experience with Christians, is a rather small sample: there are a lot more of us out here than you might think. A lot of us on the other side of that faith shift—eschewing labels and fear tactics, boundary markers and tribalist thinking.

The Church is sorting and casting off, renewing and reestablishing in the postmodern age, and this is a good thing. The old will remain—it always does—but something new is being born too. If it is being born in the Church, it is first being born in the hearts, minds, and lives of us, the Body.

Maybe evangelicalism as we understand it doesn't need defending: maybe we can open our fist, lay down our weapons for the movement or the ideology or the powerful, and simply walk away.

Labels can be helpful. Now, perhaps, they are not. Our particular tradition doesn't get our loyalty: that fidelity is for our Jesus.

Sometimes we have to cut away the old for the new to grow. We are a resurrection people, darling. God can take our death and ugliness and bitterness, our hurt and our wounds, and make something beautiful and redemptive. For you. In you. With you.

Our particular tradition doesn't get our loyalty: that fidelity is for our Jesus.

But there is never a new life, a new birth, without labor and struggle and patience, but then comes the release.

Care for the new life being born in you with tenderness. It will be tempting to take all the baggage with you—to hold on to the habits or language or rules. That's okay. You might need to be angry for a while. That's okay.

I'm not afraid for you: you are held. You are loved and you are free. I am hopeful for you.

Don't worry about the "should do" stuff anymore. It might help to cocoon away for a while, far from the performances or the structures or even the habits or thinkers that bring you pain. The Holy Spirit isn't restricted to meeting with you only in a one-hour quiet time or an official 501-3(c) tax-approved church building.

Set out, pilgrim. Set out into the freedom and the wandering. Find your people. God is much bigger, wilder, more generous, and more wonderful than you imagined.

On the other side of your wilderness, you may even find yourself reclaiming it all—the tradition, the habits, the language. You may be surprised some-

Set out, pilgrim. Set out into the freedom and the wandering.

day to find yourself right back where you began, but with new eyes, a new heart, a new mind, a new life, and a wry smile.

Now, instead of being whatever label you preferred, perhaps you can simply be a disciple, a pilgrim, out on the Way, following in the footsteps of the man from Nazareth.

You aren't condemned to wander forever. Remember now: after the wilderness comes deliverance.

* * *

It's not that all my frustrations with Church are over and done, a chapter closed. I still struggle with Church, both in the micro and the macro—with what she is and what she could be, with who we are and who we could be. There are parts of the Church that make me want to deny membership three times over before the rooster crows. I want to disassociate, to stake my claim as "not them," and identify myself as the opposite of their beliefs or ideals or passions. I'm the Pharisee, standing in the temple, loudly proclaiming in my prayers that I'm so glad I'm not a sinner like those others also standing here for mercy.

Sometimes I wonder what in the world Jesus was thinking with this church thing. It's all at sixes and sevens. It's a disaster. Talk about an inefficient way to change the world.

* * *

My husband and I were both burned out and broken, but we somehow went in different directions. These were the years of disunity between us, particularly around church.

I railed against institutions and organizations, wouldn't darken the door of a "real" church, became fluent in fault-finding and cynicism, and the word *orthodoxy* made my left eye twitch. But he tacked hard the other way, steering toward seminary, conservative denominations, structures, authorities, a longing for accountability after the Wild West, Lone Ranger atmosphere of

I became fluent in faultfinding and cynicism.

our lawless charismatic church past. I couldn't go to church without anxiety, and he couldn't fathom walking away from the work he had prepared his entire life to do.

Many of our friends and acquaintances saw my wonderings and wanderings as a liability to my husband's calling. They felt bad for him; I was holding him back. Why couldn't I fall in line? I knew this and I felt bad for him too. And those on "my side" couldn't understand why he was going back into the old ways of titles and traditions when God was moving as a fresh wind, beyond boundaries and walls and institutions.

But we were moving toward each other, as if in an ellipse. We started at the same point and then swung wide out and apart from each other before skating toward each other again. It took a while. He moved, and I moved, and God was moving. Today, we stand together, all these years later, in harmony and in step, in agreement, oneness, even in the places where we disagree (still) (yes, still) (always).

I look back on that season of our marriage, the season when we were *so* different, and I remember my husband telling me that we could give each other the gift of time and space and the room to change without fear.

I have been a dozen women in the sixteen years we've been together; he's kept pace with them all. I have kept pace with all his incarnations in return. Instead of fearing the inevitable changes that come with being a person alive in the world, we decided we would do the changing together. Anyone who gets to the end of their life with the exact same beliefs and opinions as they had at the beginning is doing it wrong.

> *Anyone who gets to the end of their life with the exact same beliefs and opinions as they had at the beginning is doing it wrong.*

But Brian and I didn't feel an urgency to convince each other. I didn't feel the need to make Brian believe and think in my ways. I understood why he was where he was. And he gave me the same grace. He even gave me the extra measure: his blessing to explore my struggles and ideas and weaknesses in a public forum through blogging about it or talking about it. He was not threatened by my honesty.

We each let the other be wrong for a long time.

* * *

I think the Church is one of the weirdest ideas and one of the best ideas.

If church were just a sanctified social club, I'd be out. If it were just about singing songs or listening to a great sermon, I could do that at home—thanks to the new worship movement albums on iTunes and free podcasts. If it were just about staying busy, I've already got that handled rather nicely.

So I've done my best to figure out the essence of the Church. I think one of the best moves we can make as a community is to shift away from a church-centered view of ourselves toward a God-centered view of us all.

A God-centered view puts the Church into its proper place within the larger context of the mission of God. God has always been "on mission" to restore and heal creation."[2] And God's mission is carried out by those He *sends.* In Genesis 12, God called Abram to be blessed and then *sent* him so that "all peoples on earth will be blessed" (NIV). This initial promise reaches its climax in the incarnation of Jesus. Jesus is *sent* by the Father into the world to save it (John 3:16). At the day of Pentecost, the Holy Spirit is *sent* to empower the believers to be witnesses. The Church is *sent* because of God's nature: He is a missionary God, a sending God. After all, the Father *sent* the Son, and the Father and the Son *sent* the Spirit, together the Trinity *sends* the Church out into the world. Jürgen Moltmann agrees: "It is not the church that has a mission of salvation to fulfill in their world; it is a mission of the Son and Spirit through the Father that includes the church."[3] Mission, then, should be understood not as one of many activities of the Church but rather as our very essence.[4] The Church is missional because it is the continuation of the mission of Christ as sent by God to the world. As Jesus instructed His disciples after His resurrection, "As the Father has sent me, I am sending you."[5]

> *I've done my best to figure out the essence of the Church.*

* * *

The Church at origin is Spirit-breathed. The grand theme of the book of Acts is that the Church is able to be a witness to the Kingdom of God because of the power of the Holy Spirit. The disciples became witnesses after the Holy Spirit fell on

The Church at origin is Spirit-breathed.

them,[6] and the Church became a witness; they began to expand their witness throughout the world. And today, it is the Holy Spirit who gathers the

people of God into community. It is through the Holy Spirit that the people of God are *sent* to continue the life and ministry of Christ.[7]

Easier said than done, right? Yes, a renewed theological understanding of the Church as a Holy Spirit gathered-and-sent community is right on. But that understanding is the easy part. Living that ideal in our current context, in the midst of a congregation or community, is just a tad more difficult.

There's a tension in the Church—and in me—between the divine essence and the human composition. In *After Our Likeness: The Church as the Image of the Trinity,* Miroslav Volf looks at this tension between human control and Spirit control within the institutions of the Church. He articulates a common view that I witnessed in the happy-clappy churches of my youth: "the Spirit of God and church institutions stand in contradiction."[8] A sort of "Holy Spirit anarchy" would be the only acceptable form for a Spirit-led church.[9] However, this fails to account for the human character that exists as people are gathered together by the Spirit. Volf goes on to argue that this view neglects "the inner essence of the church as a communion with the Triune God; an exclusively Trinitarian grounding would, by contrast, fail to do justice to the character of the church as a human community on its way to its goal."[10] Sure, we need to define the essence of the Church through God, but we can't forget that we're also a very human community. And that's good too.

The way we do church is often called "the form" or institution. So while God is responsible for its essence, as Charles Ringma wrote, "We are significantly responsible for its form."[11] To be "significantly responsible" does not mean that we take control. Rather, it means church leaders must confirm that every form lines up with the essence of the Church.[12]

The leader's role, then, is not to take control of the growth of the Church, but rather to equip the church (its present reality) to *be* the Church (its future hope). The concern should be to empower people to be who they are—representatives of the kingdom of God.[13]

We do not work toward external objectives of the Kingdom of God, but rather, we are the means of the Kingdom of God—we *are* the foretaste, the beginning of the presence of His kingdom. We should not make plans to "build" the kingdom and then include God as an appended blessing to those plans. Rather, we must work to establish God's end so His ends are represented by our means.[14]

> *The concern should be to empower people to be who they are—representatives of the kingdom of God.*

My experiences with the Church have often felt program-driven, a tail-wagging-the-dog kind of thing. We trust in our techniques in order to achieve "success"—which too often means a certain number of attendees or a line item on the budget. However, in Christ's Church, the opposite is true—we are only the Church when we submit control to the Spirit, truly representing the reign of God by embodying the new creation. Perhaps that's where we trip up: we focus so much on the forms of church, on techniques, that we forget the essence.

The other hard part is that getting church right isn't a one-and-done deal; it's what Guder calls "a continuing conversion."[15] This is crucial because "in some way [the church] is always conforming to this world and needs to be transformed by the renewal of its mind (Rom. 12:2)."[16] The Church must continue to evaluate itself, and if need be, change its structures to help the people more fully become the Church. That is, to help us become more completely who we are.[17]

Thus change in the Church is not simply God's prerogative; it is also ours. But there can be no doubt that when we acknowledge that essence and form belong together and that God's intention and our structures should harmonize—and then work for change accordingly—that God's Spirit will be actively involved in such a process.[18]

After all, before the Church is anything else, it is the Spirit's.

* * *

I go to church. Yes, the actual small-*c*, pay-your-tithe, teach-Sunday-school plain old church. I'm a church lady.

God restored me to church or church to me, I'm not sure which. Probably it's a bit of both.

I still have a lot of questions. I still get the hives when I see big churches with big splashy programs, or any mention of a building project. Talk of business plans and marketing, gimmicks and light shows make my eyes cross. Sometimes I still go to a church and feel like running, pell-mell, tumble-bumble, into the fresh air. I still love to skip Sundays just to stay home, and I don't feel guilty one little bit.

But when it was time, it was time. I suppose that's why I'm hesitant to impose timelines or rules on the journey of others. I'm hesitant to say that the way God met me and healed me will mirror someone else's journey. Claiming someone else's redemption story as a castoff that you hope will fit you is a recipe for disaster.

But one day, six years into that detox from institutional religion and with a long list of very sound and well-reasoned arguments for why I was over it, we went to a local church for Easter Sunday as a concession to convention. And all I knew was that I felt like I was home.

So we just kept showing up. The people were nice, but it wasn't like it was that different from anywhere else. We made a few friends, no big "soul mate" moments. I hatched a master plan to make friends by volunteering for a thing here and there (it worked). Some months we didn't go even once to the Sunday service. Other months, we didn't miss a week. The tinies loved every Sunday in those early days, begged to go back. They don't carry an ounce of the baggage about the gathering of the believers that their parents carted around. I got together with some of the women now and again: sometimes we became friends, other times we didn't, but that was okay somehow. I did find friends, moments of laughter and connection. I was learning how to be the same person in every corner of my life—no more masks, no more hiding my questions, my journey, my realness. It was all out there, and life became seamless. I went

> *I was learning how to be the same person in every corner of my life.*

to Bible study, the women prayed for one another, and it felt real, like everything I'd been wanting and yearning for—a bit of a mess and so full of Love. I made friends. We began to care about people; we began to feel cared for.

It took me a year to realize that I was going to church again. God had restored me to community somehow. It was sneaky, but now here it was, a gift.

For Easter every year, we set up an actual old rugged cross. It's covered in chicken wire, the beams are old and knotted, and it towers above all of us with a crude but solid base. The first time I saw it, I thought it was the weirdest and ugliest thing I'd ever seen—a harsh, unrelenting reminder. But at the end of our worship service, here is what we do as a community: we cover that old rugged cross in blossoms. We thread tulips and daisies and chrysanthemums through the chicken wire, and when we are done, that cross is blooming with new life, beauty out of bedlam and barrenness.

I love it. I love every messy, imperfect, celebratory, powerful, soulful, emotional, and wild thing about our Easters. I love our pastors, our teachers, our sound team, our choir, our children, our grandparents. I love every person who comes through the doors, I love the folding chairs, and I love the cross front and center, towering with color and beauty. I love knowing I will see some of these folks during the week, at the library, at the park, on Facebook, at Bible study, at soccer games, for a Monday night girls' night. Somehow, when I wasn't looking for it, when I gave up on ever finding it or even caring about it anymore, God made something beautiful out of my baggage, out of my brokenness, out of my church drama, my own sticky pride.

Jesus snuck up on me, surprised me with grace and community and family, a glimpse of something good, a restoration unsought.

I think if I had planned or orchestrated it, I would have missed it. I stumbled back in and found my roots growing down deep before I realized what had happened.

Jesus snuck up on me, surprised me with grace and community and family.

I am back at church because I began to figure out that all the people I loved most, the ones who were quietly doing the work of the Gospel, who were peacemakers, who were people of love and grace and mercy, *they* were the Church. I was part of the Church. We all were part of the Church if we claimed Jesus as Master. I didn't need to pretend allegiance to everything, but I did need to be part of a community. I stopped thinking macro about Church and started to think micro. I let go of my modern ideals of control and sank right into the grassroots theology of place. I practiced the radical spiritual art of staying put.

It's beautiful to me now, both the ideal and the reality. I choose the reality and I choose the ideal: I hold them both. I believe in ministering within imperfect structures. I believe in teaching Sunday school and chaperoning youth lock-ins, in carpooling seniors and vacuuming the vestry. I believe in church libraries and "just checking on you" phone calls, in the mundane daily work that creates a community on purpose. I believe in taking college girls out for coffee, in showing up at weddings, in bringing enchiladas to new mothers, in hospital committees, in homemade dainties at the funeral reception. I believe we don't give enough credit to the ones who

I stopped thinking macro about Church and started to think micro.

stay put in slow-to-change structures and movements because they change within relationship, because they take a long and a high view of time. I believe in the ones who do the whole elder board and deacon election thing, in the ones who argue for church constitutional changes and consensus building. This is not work for the faint of heart.

I believe the work of the ministry is often misunderstood, the Church is a convenient scapegoat. Heaven knows, church has been my favorite nebulous nonentity to blame, a diversionary tactic from the mirror perhaps.

A lot of people in my generation might be giving up on Church, but there are a lot of us returning, redefining, reclaiming Church too. We aren't foolish or blind or unconcerned or uneducated or unthinking. We have weighed our choices, more than anyone will know. We are choosing this and we will keep choosing each other. And sometimes our way of understanding or "doing" church looks very different, but we're still here.

I know some of us are meant to go, some are meant to stay, and most of us do a bit of both in a lifetime.

Jesus doesn't belong to church people. But church people belong to Him, in Him, and through Him.

I hope we all wrestle. I hope we look deep into our hearts and sift through our theology, our methodology, our praxis, our ecclesiology, all of it. I hope we get angry and that we say true things. I hope we push back against celebrity and consumerism; I hope we live into our birthright as a prophetic outpost for the Kingdom. I hope we get our toes stepped on and then forgive. I hope we

Jesus doesn't belong to church people. But church people belong to Him, in Him, and through Him.

become open-hearted and open-armed. I hope we are known as the ones who love.

I hope we change. I hope we grow. I hope we push against the darkness and let the light in and breathe into the Kingdom come. I hope we become a refuge for the weary and the pilgrim, for the child and the aged, for the ones who have been strong too long. And I hope we all live like we are loved.

I hope we all become a bit more inclined to listen, to pray, to wait.

I went for a walk in the wilderness for many years, and I still love it out there. I still like the fresh wind in my hair. I go for a walk every now and again, to hear God clearly in the wild spaces. I've always liked a little room to breathe. But I came home. I always come home.

I have learned to love the Church, perhaps because the Church has so beautifully loved me.

I have learned to love the Church, perhaps because the Church has so beautifully loved me. I love the Church in all the places I find her now—cathedrals and living rooms, monasteries and mega-churches, school gymnasiums and warehouses.

* * *

When I think about the whole big institution of marriage, it can seem a bit overwhelming—the whole "for as long as you both shall live" part, the idea of linking our lives together without knowledge of the future or the ways our lives will unfold. We aren't guaranteed any particular outcome. It's a choice for a life of selflessness and mutuality, a decision to love and play second fiddle to each other, a laying down of one's own way and an embrace of never-ending compromise. Then there is the big theological understanding of the sacrament of marriage, the way that our marriages represent the communal God, the way we are a picture of Christ and the Church, the way we embody some metaphors of the Spirit. It's a lot to carry, a lot to sign up for in the abstract.

I didn't marry my husband because I wanted to get married in the abstract. I wanted to marry *Brian*.

He didn't marry me because he believed in the sanctity of marriage or thought it was necessary for His career path or because it seemed like a logical step. In fact, both of us had plans in the abstract to delay marriage. He was planning on a life lived in Christian service in Mexico; I was planning to write for a few years in a flat in London. Neither of us wanted to get married. We had big dreams and big plans instead. Marriage in the abstract would only complicate those plans; we were under no illusions.

> *I didn't marry my husband because I wanted to get married in the abstract. I wanted to marry* Brian.

But instead, here is what happened: we went on a date to a burger joint, and next thing we knew, we were slow-dancing to old Garth Brooks songs on the AM radio on a back road in Tulsa. And then after that, who cared about the plans and the dreams? Our only plans and dreams were each other. There was no sacrifice, no second thought. We might not have picked the life we had in the abstract, but in the very specific, this would be our choice a thousand times over. When the big was overwhelming, the small choice of us was perfect sense, an easy "of course." Getting married was the most natural, most straightforward path. It wasn't the expected path—but it was our path, we were sure of that. Not because we wanted marriage, but because we wanted *each other*.

I didn't want to embody marriage, I wasn't thinking of how great it would be for life and ministry and theological teaching. I simply wanted to wake up beside him every day for the rest of my life. I wanted to have babies with him. I wanted to kiss him up against the washing machine. I wanted to grow old with him. I wanted to fight with him and for him. I wanted to balance budgets. I wanted to entwine our lives until we were one. I wanted him. I still feel that way. I don't want to be *a* wife, I want to be *Brian's* wife.

I think that way about Church sometimes. Abstracts are a bit overwhelming. Some days, I don't sign up for the whole big institutional abstract or ideal thing of Church: that feels overwhelming. But I do entwine my life with our local church, our community: this is something I can do. I go small, I choose reality, I choose the daily mess of an actual place and actual people over the abstracts.

I don't want to be a wife, I want to be Brian's wife.

And yet . . . our marriage does embody our theology. Being the Church on a small scale does give a sign and a foretaste of the Kingdom of God. The more committed I am to the local church, the more I see it happening in us and through us: the metaphor makes more sense because the universal has become so beautifully particular.

Sometimes we are living out the big metaphors rather effortlessly, in the end.

* * *

So why do I go to church?

Because we drive by the farms on the edge of town and the tinies watch for sheep. Because I almost always consider pulling over on the side of the road just to take photos of our Sunday drive: the crisp blue sky and the sharp green rolling hills, the turning-red blueberry bushes squatted across the fields, the rise of the mountains in the haze of morning. But how can you Instagram the rush of cold air in your lungs and how it makes you feel so beautifully, so fully, alive?

Because we walk in and Pat hugs me while she hands a bulletin to my son, Joe. Because after a week of Facebook and school pick-up and drop-off lines, a week of writing and laundry, a week of working and to-do lists, I hear my name called out in the lobby and, for that moment, someone sees me. Because we laugh with one friend, ask how another one's health is doing, figure out who needs a meal this week. We exchange quick hugs as placeholders for the conversation that might unfold this week or next, maybe next month. We engage in all the small talk that precedes the heart talks. Because my tinies head for the kid table of coloring pages and crayons and offer up a high five to the children's pastor. Because we sit in folding chairs in a rather drafty school gym and our tinies sprawl on the floor at our feet or perch on our hips or stand beside us and watch it all, all, all, taking it in.

Because my friend Tracy leads worship while wearing biker boots, and sometimes her hair is pink. Because when she stomps those boots on that wooden stage and when she stretches her arms out wide, tips her head back, and cries out to God like she believes it, it makes me want to sit down

We engage in all the small talk that precedes the heart talks.

and cry. Because my son wants to sit in the front row. Because my toddler raises her hands up and warbles and hollers a song, and no one gives her a dirty look. Because my eldest is twirling in the back with her best friends, waving flags.

Because that couple over there just got married and that other one has been married for forty years. Because that man wearing total dad-khakis has his arm around his teenage son, and because that lady took my exhausted friend's little baby right out of her arms and said, *Go on, you go on and sing or sit down. I'll look after her for a little while.* And I saw my friend's eyes well up with thankful tears. Because this guy is in recovery and that guy is his sponsor.

Because I love to sing, and where else do we get to sing communally anymore? Because I love happy-clappy choruses and sober hymns, because "I love you, Lord" sounds so beautiful in my own mouth. Because I love to worship with my people, and these are my people.

Because I sit beside my husband and we whisper back and forth during the sermon; it's the closest we get to date night some months. Because we know and love our pastors for their humanity, not in spite of it, because of the way they show up for us. Because sometimes it's an amazing sermon and sometimes it's, um, not. Because we pass the bread and the cup, and we give each other communion, and there is room at the table for everyone in this room.

Because even though the phrase "going to church" kind of bugs me (we don't *go*, we *are*), and even though it's messy and imper- *There is room at the table* fect, even though I've let them down *for everyone in this room.* and they have let me down, even though there are disappointments, even though I don't agree with everybody and they probably think I'm crazy sometimes too, even though I don't think we need an official sanctioned Sunday morning thing to be part of the Body of Christ, I keep choosing this small family out of hope and joy.

Because it frustrates me. Because I often kick against convention and conformity while crying out for community, because I need the refinement of my edges, because I need a place to practice it all together. Because this time, I came into it knowing I would be disappointed by these people and that I would disappoint them, but I decided before it ever happened what I was going to do with that disappointment: I was going to see it through.

Because I want my children to grow up with the imperfect community of God like I did. Because I want to reclaim my heritage of faith as worthy of intention. Because I need to receive and I need to give. Because I want the tinies to know that however much I mess up, however much I fall short of my own ideals, I was planted in the house of God because this is where I practice it, learn it, start it all over again. Because I want my tinies to know what my voice sounds like when I sing "Amazing Grace."

Because we gather with the full knowledge that we're being sent back out, a sent community by a sending God, all for the redemption, rescue, and renewal of the world.

Because at the end of the service, we practice the priesthood of all believers and anyone can pray for anyone else. *Just go ahead and pray, go ahead. Talk to each other, you don't need a sanctioned commissioning, you are already part of this Body, so go on then.*

Because I know Jesus better when I hear about Him from other people who follow Him too. Because I almost always encounter the Holy Spirit in a profound, sideways sort of way when we're gathered together in His name.

Because some of my greatest wounds have come from church, and so my greatest healing has happened here too.

In a fractured and mobile and hypercustomized world, intentional community—plain old church—feels like a radical act of faith and sometimes like a spiritual discipline. We show up at a rented school and drink a cup of tea with the people of God.

Some of my greatest wounds have come from church, and so my greatest healing has happened here too.

And we remember together who we are and why we live this life, and we figure out all over again how to be disciples of the Way.

Be a Person

ON COMMUNITY AND FRIENDSHIP

You sent out the e-mails with the place and the time. You stopped at the grocery store for bread and a bottle of the finest grape juice. Serving real wine for communion isn't as important as welcoming the ones to the table too who can't or won't drink wine.

That night, you bathed all the tinies and put them in their beds early. You realized the washroom needed a quick wipe-down and madly ran around with a rag. You set out the mugs for tea. The door is unlocked. Everyone can just walk right in. They know that.

You covered your beat-up old coffee table with a table-cloth from the thrift store. You arranged candles, laid out your Bible and your Common Prayer. You placed the bread and the juice, and—just like that—you turned your coffee table into an altar. And that is how the gathering begins on a rainy Thursday night in a small city in the West.

You love the way the men make each other laugh, the way their faces crinkle at the eyes. You love the way the women congregate in the kitchen so easily, standing around talking about their days. As the group gathers in the living room, conversation begins with logistics and scheduling, then moves to a few frustrations, then prayer, conversation, world affairs and affairs closer to home, then silence as prayer. Refill the kettle, we're here for a while yet.

It's dark outside, pouring rain. Your babies are sleeping in their beds under the quilts their grandma made for them, miraculously snoring through the loud laughter. The candles on your homemade altar drip drip drip as the night unfolds, and this is your church, these are your people. They look you in the eye. You know their stories, they know yours, but there is still so much to discover. Hope is hard-won and present.

And then you—yes, you—you pray over their bowed heads, each one so precious, and invite them to the table.

So come to this table,
you who have much faith
and you who would like to have more;
you who have been here often
and you have not been here for a long time;
you who have tried to follow Jesus,
and you who have failed;
come. It is Christ who invites us to meet Him here.[1]

You tear off the bread and hand it to your friend: *This is His body, broken for you.* Then she turns and hands it to the man beside her, blesses him with that same benediction. Then you pass the cup—*This is His blood, spilled for you*—and you all partake together, one after another, hand to hand. You aren't standing in a line, you're beside each other, and it's hard not to grin. Together, you read Scripture out of the book of Isaiah, and right now, right here you are looking at the way the desert has bloomed. This is your river running to Zion, and it's right here in your own living room. Then it's *Good night, good night. I'm so glad I was here, I'm so glad you could come, this was just what I needed. I love you, love you too. See you next week.*

This is another way to fall back in love with the Bride of Christ: open your doors and welcome her into your life.

* * *

Churches have really gotten into the word *community* lately. I'm glad for that. It's important to make sure people don't fall through the cracks and that as a body we have a way of making sure we see each other. But in our rush to do so, we can take the Spirit out of community. We modernize it, quantify it, formalize it, and assign people to groups. We think we can arrange community. Or we think that because people are in the same stage of life, they will be friends—young marrieds, singles, mothers of young children, men, whatever grouping is in vogue at the moment. Sometimes these methods work out beautifully and we find our community there, but sometimes the magic just isn't there. The groups may feel forced and manufactured; rushed relationships are rarely real relationships. It takes time to find our community, doesn't it?

Sometimes they go to our church, sometimes they don't. I find my deepest relationships are ones that

Rushed relationships are rarely real relationships.

develop over time, over the discipline of staying put and showing up, of sharing stories slowly as they unfold with each earned moment of trust, of listening, of being a person.

Ah, being a person. That sounds like such an odd phrase, I know, but I use it all the time to remind myself that it's holy work to be a person, that this is how we build community, how we become friends. Our world seeks to dehumanize us or reduce us to our talking points or our politics, our labels or our bank accounts or our dress size.

It's tempting to be a defender of an institution. Or an office, a title. We like to be the oracle or the activist, the self-help manual or an encyclopedia or a concordance or a few tactical probing questions to steer the conversation. Some of us are the faultfinders. A select few are the heroes or cops or gatekeepers.

I believe our most sacred moments are often our most human moments.

So when it comes to how we do community—to the building of it, the maintaining of it, the creating of it, whatever—I'm not really into the whole tactics or steps or strategic plans. Just be a person. We should say out loud: you are not alone and I am here. I think community is healthiest when we are fully human, alive in Christ, and alive to one another. As Jean Vanier writes, "Community is a sign that love is possible in a materialistic world where people so often either ignore or fight each other. It is a sign that we don't need a lot of money to be happy—in fact, the opposite."[2] We are more than our opinions.

* * *

When I stopped going to church, I didn't know how to make friends anymore.

When your entire friendship network revolves around church, it's disorienting to step outside the system. Even the friends who want to stay in touch with us simply can't: so much of friendship relies upon our joint participation in gathering together at a particular place or event. If we don't go to the Bible studies or show up on Sunday mornings or help to teach Sunday school, we miss out on the moments of our friends' lives and they miss out on ours. It's that simple even if it is sad.

When I stopped going to church, I was lonely. I can't lie about that.

But it can be just as lonely inside the building as out. I know this too well. When we are lonely, people will often tell us to "get plugged into" a church. But that's rarely enough. Just showing up on Sunday morning, as part of a crowd, doesn't cure loneliness, and it doesn't create community, let alone friendship.

When I stopped going to church, I didn't know how to make friends anymore.

There are a lot of reasons people go to church—to participate in corporate worship, to receive good teaching, to pray with and for others, or because we feel that Scripture demands it of us. But a big reason many of us show up on a Sunday morning is that we also want to be part of a village. We go to church because that is how we know to build our community: we need someone to love us and show up in our lives. And I don't think that's a less holy reason than any other; it's a very real and legitimate need, and a church community is a real and legitimate way to meet that need.

But when I took an unplanned six years off from official church stuff, I had to figure out a community on my own. I remember having an emotional breakdown when I was near to giving birth to one of the tinies, crying because we had "no community." But then, in the days after her birth, I began to realize that we had built a community in our own way.

Dave and Jamie across the street brought a full supper over. Another neighbor brought chocolates and stuffed animals. My friend Sarah brought over stickers for the tinies as well as flowers and a Starbucks card for me. My husband's coworker's wife brought over a full roast chicken dinner complete with a bucket of cookies, and his office-mate dropped off a vat of chili. His boss came by with food and baby jammies. Even my friends around the world made sure I was going to the post office almost every day to pick up another package with hand-scrawled notes of congratulations, baby socks, and gift cards. People from our neighborhood or from our workplaces made sure that we had flowers, cards, and adorable baby sleepers everywhere. I didn't cook for three weeks because my freezer and fridge were completely stocked.

Church people don't have exclusive rights to looking after others. It turns out that you can find community in the craziest places. Like in the midst of your life—as it is right now. In our normal lives, our getting-up-and-walking-around lives, Brian and I somehow built a village. I hadn't see it before because I wasn't driving ten minutes to see them religiously every Sunday. But there they were, loving us, and we loved all of them too.

It turned out that when you spend your afternoons outside in the neighborhood, the neighborhood knows who you are. When you hang out on your driveway to pass the time with every dog who gets walked past, the dog owners look forward to it. When you sit on the front steps and watch all the neighborhood kids play with your kids, their parents sooner or later come outside too.

So maybe it's not formal. Maybe it doesn't have a nonprofit status. Maybe it doesn't count as "going to church." We drop food at someone's house when they're sick; no leader organized it. We just do it because this is what we do. This is being a person in a community.

I like it. I like the decentralized, informal living out of community. Sometimes I think that *community* is just a churchy word for the old-fashioned goodness of being a friend. I like being led by the Spirit and not by my obligations or guilt or fear or the "practical ministry schedule." I like listening to God speak through regular people. I like the flat structure of an organic community, our you-too-me-too conversation. So even though I'm a proper church lady again, I've found that community can exist both inside and outside of an institutional church.

* * *

I have to admit though: sometimes all the talk about "community" in the Church freaks me out. Not just because of the implied expectation of constant togetherness or the pressure to feel guilty for my beloved solitary pursuits like quiet weekends and walking or reading or writing. As the old joke goes, "Introverts, unite! (Preferably separately.)" It's also the way that it can make us feel like *everyone* should have full and unrestricted access to our time, energy, spirit, and soul.

A few friends and I were recently chatting about that buzzword—*community*—and trying to figure out why it felt weird. While we talked about our own best and worst experiences, my friend Amber rather casually mentioned that we just aren't meant for community with five hundred people. This rang true for me because it articulated how I manage my own quest for community and friendship, expectations and intimacy.

Some folks think we need to be vulnerable and transparent and deeply connected with everyone and their dog and Facebook and our church. But that's just not so. Brené Brown says we should only share with people who have earned the right to hear our story.[3] We're not made for friendship promiscuity. That's not community anyway, that's just casting our pearls before swine, and it's probably a profanity to our souls.

Community isn't an exercise in consumerism and gluttony. Community is not *more + more + more = better.*

I picture my relationships like concentric circles, progressively getting smaller and smaller.[4]

The Crowd is on the biggest outside circle. These are the people with whom I don't have any real intimacy—people I know by name or sight through church or the neighborhood, perhaps through blogging or social media or school pickups.

Community isn't an exercise in consumerism and gluttony.

We run in the same circles, but we're not really much more than acquaintances. And that's okay. The entire church is not my community, just as the entire city is not my community.

The next smallest circle is My Community. These are the people with whom I have a measure of real, reciprocal friendship or shared life. We've committed to a common core in some way, and we have become friends. One friend of mine explained that community is the circle that encompasses our relationship somehow—a church, a shared faith, a shared vocation, that sort of thing. I just can't say "community" without thinking it requires a measure of friendship and loyalty. These are the people who require commitment from me. I enjoy our time together, absolutely, but I've also *decided* to love them and decided to do life with them, and so now I act like it by showing up and by being committed to our friendship. I have several communities—my church, my neighborhood, even my online community at my blog or my Facebook page. I might not share my deepest, darkest secrets, but there is a trust there, reciprocity of relationship.

Then there are My Somewheres. We all need somewhere to say the private things, the vulnerable things, the scary and true things, the victories and the defeats. "I need to say it *some-where*," we say. So then the temptation is to say everything, everywhere, or we end up saying nothing, nowhere. There's something between oversharing or undersharing our real lives. I have learned—slowly, painfully—to say these private things to my Somewheres.

In times of conflict or difficulty, I tend to withdraw—big-time. I pull deeply inward and don't emerge until I've settled whatever has been ailing me, until I have developed a nice story with a bow on the top. This is the great frustration of the ones who love me, I hear. I withdraw, I shut down, I retreat in times of conflict—both external and internal.

So this is my learned spiritual discipline: I talk to my Somewheres. I say discipline because that is what it takes for me to reach out during conflict. It takes intentional discipline to be honest while I'm still in the midst of the unfinished struggle. I have to say the words out loud: here are my contradictions. I don't always do it well.

Funnily enough, I can be even more reluctant to share my victories than I am to share my imperfections. The universal Canadian love-language is self-deprecation. And yet sometimes cool things happen, amazing things even, and I have found I need somewhere to unapologetically brag too.

The Somewheres are my cure for the Everywhere and the Nowhere. Neither extreme is good for our souls. We can't say everything to everyone. It's foolish and damaging to expose ourselves to every single person with an opinion, to let just anyone's criticism or direction come to rest heavily on our stories.

And we can't keep our contradictions all in either, or we will be crushed, eventually. I think our souls require some release: for wisdom, for perspective, for laughter, for tears, for even the holy act of hearing, "I see you and I'm listening." We need to receive from one another, receive the gifts that God has placed before us in our right-now lives. Paul wrote of this in Galatians 6:2 when he encouraged us to "bear one another's burdens and so fulfill the law of Christ." We need each other. People get a bit squirrelly when they refuse to lay down their masks. No one should be above getting their mail read.

"I need to say it somewhere. And you're my Somewhere," I said to my friends. And so we embraced the word, this idea of being each other's Somewhere. We are the Somewheres for an unapologetic brag or a tearful admission or a "here's the whole story behind this thing" or a disappointment or frustration in every corner of our lives. We all need somewhere to say that your heart is broken and you can't get your baby to sleep and you wonder if you're wasting your life and your marriage isn't doing so good and you feel alive for the first time and you are tired and you heard a terrible joke you can't wait to tell someone and you found a new paint color for your bedroom and your teenager is giving you attitude and you want to sell everything you own to move to Paris but this time you mean it.

I have found too that good Somewheres listen and see, but they also push back and challenge. As the writer of Hebrews said, we "stir up one another to love and good works" (10:24 ESV). We will become truly human when we are truly communal, for we're made in the image of God, a communal Trinity God. Some part of our soul starves in isolation and in anonymous crowds. The best relationships are reciprocal, an intentional but unchoreographed give-and-take.

I believe we can be authentic in our lives. I do. I hope I am authentic. I hope my life is seamless, transparent even. I long to be the same person online as I am off-line, in church as I am in my neighborhood, at work as I am in my family, in "real life" as I am in my books. I believe we can speak our truth and own our truth and unapologetically write it, share it, speak it, live it. I think it's best to live as if there is no such thing as a secret, sure. And I believe that while we're doing that, going through our lives unarmed and with our hearts broken and our hands open, that we still need—perhaps even more—a Somewhere, a safe refuge, a place to work out what is working in us. We can't be everything to everyone, so why should everyone receive everything that we are? Henri Nouwen writes, "We probably have wondered in our many lonesome moments if there is one corner in this competitive, demanding world where it is safe to be released, to expose ourselves to someone else, and to give unconditionally. It might be very small and hidden. But if this corner exists, it calls for a search through the complexities of our human relationships in order to find it."[5]

Here are a few things you need to become Somewheres: An ability to welcome the contradictions in each other. Ferocious trust. Secret-keeping. A shared sense of humor. A fierce belief in the inherent goodness and holiness of each other. An equal amount of butt kicking and hair petting. Bravery. Silliness. A common core. The capacity to laugh through tears. A "you're not telling the truth" detector. An aversion to the phrase, "I'm fine." Unconditional welcome. Time, so much time. Openness to being challenged. A lot of small and inconsequential talk to lay the foundation for the big scary talks. Loyalty like blood. Showing up at the right time. Light for the darkness. And then there is the part you can't predict or plan or program: magic. There needs to be a bit of that Holy Spirit drawing together, a sense of purpose and destiny, an answered prayer, a shared language, all your own, discovered at last.

The ways we connect with each other may be quite typical—Sunday morning services or school pickups or school or work or afternoon walks or Bible studies at church. Or more typical to our generation—Facebook, Twitter, texting. Either way, we don't feel quite so alone in our moments of choosing brave. We feel seen, we feel heard, we feel prayer at our back and a community waiting up ahead of us on the path.

We don't feel quite so alone in our moments of choosing brave.

Even with My Somewheres, I have a handful, a small handful, of friendships that are deeper and more daily. Within that circle, there is a teeny-tiny circle of my closest ones. We have free range in each other's lives.

My friend Kristin—who is one of My Somewheres—references these circles far more spiritually than I do. She says that Jesus had the Crowd, then He had His large group of Followers, then his Disciples, then the Twelve, then just the Three—John, Peter, and James—who went into the Garden with him while He prayed before His crucifixion. So Kristin calls her most intimate circle her "Garden Friends"—the people she would want with her in the garden before death, standing watch with her. I like her way of looking at it.

* * *

I hate conflict. I am a conflict avoider. I tend to confuse the absence of conflict with peace. But now I've learned that peacemaking often involves a bit of healthy conflict: we're not called to be peacekeepers but peacemakers.

A while ago, I was a pretty terrible friend to someone I love very much. When I was finally called out for it, I was defensive, and an argument ensued. I reacted like a wounded animal when I was the one who had wounded my friend: it was my fault. Perhaps that's why I freaked out so thoroughly; I felt guilty and knew my friend was right. The snot was flying and nearly an hour later, I was repenting and sobbing with remorse. My friend and I followed the argument all the way down to redemption and forgiveness, and we emerged battle-worn and exhausted—and reconciled.

It was a holy moment in our friendship.

Real life is the undignified life, and it is the classroom for holiness. If you can't find God while you're changing diapers or serving food or hanging out with your friends, you won't find God at the worship service or the spiritual retreat or the regimented daily quiet time or the mission field. If you can't embrace healthy conflict, you'll never have a truly honest friendship.

I believe God hides in plain sight in your right-now life. And if you have the guts to taste and see, confront and wrestle and rest, you'll encounter the most holy—maybe most strongly when you are most uncomfortable.

I hate to break it to you, but not everything is rainbows and unicorns and cupcakes when it comes to friendship and community. One thing I've finally accepted about community is that, when done right, it's always a bit supernatural. It requires the activity of the Spirit in each of us and between us. It's not natural for us to love one another, to play second fiddle to one another, to lay down our lives for one another. It's not natural to be unselfish and giving, to put others first. So as Dietrich Bonhoeffer wrote, "Our community with one another consists solely in what Christ has done to both of us."[6] Or as John wrote, "The way we

> *I believe God hides in plain sight in your right-now life.*

know we've been transferred from death to life is that we love our brothers and sisters. Anyone who doesn't love is as good as dead." And then, "This is how we've come to understand and experience love: Christ sacrificed His life for us. This is why we ought to live sacrificially for our fellow believers, and not just be out for ourselves" (excerpted 1 John 3:14–17). We can only truly love one another in the selfless and grace-filled ways of Christ when we are living deeply within Christ.

* * *

Our faith is often embodied in the relationships and neighborhoods where we live. In our world of globalization, technology, and mobility, we've misplaced the sacredness of place.

The act of staying and living in our place has an impact on us practically, of course, but also on us theologically. It's not always sexy to stay put, is it? In most of my church tradition, no one ever mentioned the holy work of *staying*.

No one talked about how the places where we live life matter to our spiritual formation, how we are shaped by our communities, by our rootedness, our geography, by our families, and by the complex web of connections and history that emerge only by staying.

In most of my church tradition, no one ever mentioned the holy work of staying.

I used to live the Gospel beautifully in my own head; I thought about it all the time. But the radical act of staying put, a commitment to practicing a theology of place, is teaching me—the overthinker—that thinking isn't quite the same thing as *doing*. My intentions and beliefs and pontificating about community don't matter one iota if I am not engaged in living out the reality of it.

The theology of place is different from most of what I was taught in my younger days. The modern church always taught us to forsake all for the Gospel and *go*. We were more likely to celebrate the forsaking or sacrificing of home and community and friendships. We go, we move, we grow, we create destination churches and video venues, programs every night of the week, and then wonder why we don't know our neighbors or why we feel so alone.

My intentions and beliefs and pontificating about community don't matter one iota if I am not engaged in living out the reality of it.

I love the language of "place" when we talk about community because it sets my living and my rising, my working and my rhythms as a sacrament. The radical act of staying put is shaping me. Brian and I have been in this place longer than anywhere else we've lived. It took more years than I would have predicted for the emergence of community to happen, but now I go to the store and see neighbors pushing their carts up the aisle. I gather at church services and anticipate conversations with friends; I teach Sunday school to the same kids and I know them by name; I go to Canadian Tire and run into my husband's clients. The tinies look forward all year to the rituals and festivals unique to our area, like the Berry Beat Festival or the Cranberry Festival. We watch the same forest every spring for the first blossoms, our two screech owls—we named them Ron and Hermione because, well, obviously— and even the same brown bears lumber through in the late fall with regularity. Oh, the excitement when the cubs grew to lanky teenager bears right before our eyes (safely ensconced behind the windows, of course). My spiritual formation has been shaped by the lush green spring and the gray, rainy winters with long nights and short days. I am only now seeing the holy work of showing up, in praying out loud for our friends in my living room, in tending a garden, in walking the same path every day, of watching children grow up, of friendships deepened by doing life together year after year. Kurt Vonnegut once counseled, "What should young people do with their lives today? Many things, obviously. But the most daring thing is to create stable communities in which the terrible disease of loneliness can be cured."[7]

I am living my faith out, in a real way, as an embodiment of the Gospel in a real place, in a real context, with real people.

Staying put and daring to be known, engaging in life with people just as imperfect and weird as me, staying through the seasons as they come and go is changing me to be more like the Jesus I love so wildly. It's a different kind of fearless, the fearlessness of no masks, the fearlessness of engaging in community—slowly and steadily and wholeheartedly. Real, hard conversations usually only come after a lot of surface conversations.

Daily examples of Galilee peppered the teaching of our Jesus: everything from catching fish to baking bread is a sign and a foretaste of the ways of Christ and His Kingdom.

I like that. I like to think that everything from gathering the neighbor's blueberries to refereeing street hockey games, to feeding the hungry to advocating for the homeless—all of it is a sacrament of community. We can embody the Gospel by going, absolutely, but we can also embody the Gospel by our roots, by our unhurried community development, by our family meals and our wanderings. Some of us embody the Gospel by staying put.

Truly Human

ON HEAVEN AND THE KINGDOM OF GOD

Once I read a book about a child who was kidnapped (since becoming a mother, I can't read those kinds of books anymore, so this must have been many years ago). The boy was kidnapped as a toddler, and they brainwashed him. They gave him a new name, they called themselves his mum and dad, and they created an entire life for him. From the outside, it was so normal—school, baseball, family suppers—and they were satisfied that he had forgotten his old life and that this was their stolen happily ever after.

But there was still something there, buried deep in his heart; he knew that something wasn't right. He had dreams of his old life, recurring dreams of his mother and his father, his old room. And even though he was happy and his kidnappers were rather good to him, he wasn't surprised, not one bit, to eventually discover that he had been kidnapped and that his entire life had been a lie. When he finally was restored to his real home, everyone worried about how it would go, because really, they were all strangers to him. But when he saw his real mother, his real father, and his home, he wept and simply said that he always knew, he always knew, the truth was there in his heart the whole time.

I sometimes feel that way about God and us. I feel like maybe we're all exiles. We have been stolen from our real life.

We think we're in our regular life, but there is this thing, this sense, this memory of something better, something more, something that is everything good and perfect still stuck in our hearts.

And even when everything is good or we've achieved everything we ever wrote on our bucket list or pinned onto Pinterest boards or we accomplish some long list of the world's version of success and we achieve celebrity or money or the house with the kids and the dog, we still know, deep in our hearts, that we're exiles and something, something isn't right here.

It's not enough. All the stuff, all the things, all the experiences, all the good or the thrilling or sexy stuff is just a smokescreen of goodness. It's an approximation of something real to convince everyone else that we're fine, we're normal, but really, we know the whole time that we don't quite fit, we know something is off, we know we're not where we belong.

The memory of God's kingdom is there.

It's there in the stuff of the soul, the tendrils of the spirit. Like the psalmist sang, we're like those who dream of home.[1] It's submerged somewhere in our brain or our soul, perhaps, but we know, *we know*, the truth is there, in our hearts, the whole time.

The memory of God's kingdom is there.

We see glimpses of it; we have a hunch or a memory we can't quite grasp. It drifts like smoke or storms in like flashes of lightning insight or takes our breath away. We make love, we learn, we sing, we watch the stars come out, we care, we connect, we labor, we carry, we nurse, we cry, we dance—we witness restoration like we witness the night sky: it looks like a million tiny particles of light, but each one is actually bigger, more dazzling, than we could fathom.

We have these moments of transcendence, like the veil between heaven and earth is fluttering. We can't breathe for the loveliness of the world and each other, and just like that, we remember something.

We have these moments of transcendence, like the veil between heaven and earth is fluttering—and just like that, we remember something.

Our skin is made of dust, so we often catch the perfumed scent of the Garden in the cool of the evening, and we know, somewhere inside, that we're supposed to be walking with God, unashamed still.

I wonder if that's really what happens when we meet Jesus. It's not that we meet Him or that we believe in Him or that we "invite Him into our hearts" or that we mentally assent to some nonnegotiable truths that will govern our best life now.

No, I think it's that we *recognize* Him.

I think that part of our souls, our spirits, our bodies, our minds, locks into focus. It wasn't a dream, no, *that* is what's real. When we cross the threshold of faith, we enter into an awareness that the Kingdom of God has already come.

And we realize, oh, my God, I always knew, I always knew, the truth was there, in my heart, the whole time. We can't articulate it; if we tried to say it out loud it would sound foolish. So instead, the inexplicable longing resides until it is fulfilled: the Kingdom of God. Love, hope, joy, peace, kindness, all of it. This is what God intended for us. This is what we are moving toward, every day: the restoration of this beautiful home, the redemption of all of us, the rescue of all of us from the false life that we think is real. We were made for this life instead. We're home.

* * *

Sometimes during our journey, we don't realize that we are experiencing a turning point until everything in us and about us has been turned inside out. That's how this was for me.

Sometimes when we start to sort through our faith, we know exactly where we want to begin. For years, we have been eyeing that box marked Human Sexuality or Salvation or The Problem of Evil, perhaps the one labeled What I Believe about Evolution/Creation. And so when the transition comes, when the sorting begins on the threshold of our grief or our fear or our anger, we make a beeline for that box.

"Definitely this one first," we say. We roll up our sleeves and dive straight in with all the energy of a pre-Christmas purge. We know we need to sweep away the old to make room for the new. And since these specific topics have taken up so much emotional or spiritual real estate, we want to tackle them first; the questions press down upon us. We want to lay it all out and figure out what we keep and what we toss: at times our very lives depend on those answers.

We want to figure out what we keep and what we toss: at times our very lives depend on those answers.

And then there are the boxes we stumble upon in dusty corners or attics, the ones we discover under the sink. Sometimes we get a bit forgetful, after all, and then we're surprised when we come across the baggage: *Oh, here too?* we think.

Sometimes we know where our sorting waits for us. Other

times, it takes a bright light shining in, the doors swinging open wide, the curtains flying apart while the windows are pushed up and open. Sometimes the wind and the light have to sweep in before we can see into those corners. The house is beginning to smell fresh, you are beginning to feel as if you belong here now, but first, let's take a peek in the corners.

* * *

I don't think we give enough credit to the ones with questions. Oftentimes they are simply saying out loud what the rest of us are thinking or wondering. The questions aren't the threat—it's the alternative to growing numb and complacent, the specter of a stalled-out journey, the encroaching quiet desperation that terrified Thoreau,[2] or the silencing of one's true self out of fear or a need to belong.

Blessed are the wonderers with the courage to live into the questions.

   Blessed are the wonderers with the courage to live into the questions. Seems to me that sooner or later, whether we like the outcome or not, theirs is the answer.

* * *

I didn't think much about heaven beyond what I heard in church and pop culture. An ethereal vision of clouds and streets of gold, angels and mansions, perhaps. (Prosperity preachers do love to talk about the extravagance of heaven, don't they?) But now I remember a friend of mine once sharing a photo he had taken of a forest of aspens in the fall. Their leaves had turned bright gold and then fallen to the ground, carpeting his path with gold. "I wonder if maybe we need to rethink that whole 'streets of gold' thing," he said.

Those aspen leaves seemed holy to me, a street of gold for the redeemed.

* * *

The discovery of the Kingdom of God not only reoriented my faith, it drew me right back to the Church I thought I could leave out of my faith.

* * *

According to theologian Dallas Willard, the Church preaches two atonements.[3] First, there's the Gospel of Atonement, or maybe you know it as sin management: that's the one where we all get to go to heaven when we die because we make a personal confession of Jesus Christ as Lord and Savior. This is where a lot of our modern evangelism efforts have focused: the decision day, walk the aisle and say the prayer, the get-out-of-hell-free card, and the rest of our life dedicated to good behavior, an attempt to "stop sinning."

But Jesus taught something quite different: the Gospel of the Kingdom. This is discipleship, apprenticeship. Sin management makes converts, the Gospel of the Kingdom makes disciples of Jesus Christ. And there's a big difference there in how we engage in our lives.

In the Kingdom of God, we join with God in co-creation, in the work of the new earth. We love and we follow Jesus. We shape our lives into His life, to live here on earth as He would live among us. We weren't called to follow political parties or ideology, nationalism, consumerism, or power. Instead, we were called to apprentice ourselves to Jesus' way of life. We were called to be part of establishing the Kingdom of God here and now in our walking-around lives. Partnering with God to see the Kingdom come. As Willard said in *The Divine Conspiracy,* "Jesus offers Himself as God's doorway into the life that is truly life. Confidence in Him leads us today, as in other times, to become apprentices to eternal living."[4]

"I came to give you life and life more abundant,"[5] Jesus said.

* * *

I think my discovery of the difference between *converts* and *disciples*—a discovery, which, let's be clear, shouldn't have been a discovery at all—has changed me and has given me hope and direction for my life. This orthodox teaching of Christianity has seemingly been lost in all the Salvation Olympics of "soul saving" in the past fifty years.

I tend to agree with Scot McKnight's belief that "Kingdom of God" is one of the most misunderstood phrases in the Church today.[6] We either neuter it into a social gospel or reduce it to an individual salvation experience.

No, the Kingdom of God is the Church active and alive today—the disciples of Jesus in the world.

The Kingdom of God was the message of Jesus and it's the work *I am not in the business* of every believer now. This gives me *of sin management* focus and understanding for my life *anymore: instead I am* today. I am not in the business of sin *being transformed into* management anymore: instead I am *His likeness.* being transformed into His likeness.

I am an exile in this fallen and broken world, here to plant gardens and to prepare for the coming day when all things will be

renewed and restored, to tend to the earth and to humanity—
and my place in the world—with tender ferocity. We are participating in the life of Christ.

Our lives are prophesying the Kingdom of God right now.
When we follow Jesus, we are meant to be outposts for God's
way of life.

So what are our hopes? What do we believe and know about
the life that Jesus came to give us, the life more abundant?
Imagine the world fully redeemed and restored and rescued. Go
ahead. Imagine it. (And it's okay, you can weep for all the loss
and the pain and sorrow of our world as it is.) But then, we live
into that envisioned life, right now, as exiles establishing a kingdom for a soon-coming king. We use our imaginations prophetically, and then we begin to embody God's best dreams for us all.

As Brennan Manning wrote, "The gospel is absurd and the
life of Jesus is meaningless unless we believe that He lived,
died, and rose again with but one purpose in mind: to make
brand-new creation. Not to make people with better morals but
to create a community of prophets and professional lovers, men
and women who would surrender to the mystery of the fire of
the Spirit that burns within, who would live in ever greater fidelity to the omnipresent Word of God, who would enter into
the center of it all, the very heart and mystery of Christ, into the
center of the flame that consumes, purifies, and sets everything
aglow with peace, joy, boldness, and extravagant, furious love.
This, my friend, is what it really means to be a Christian."[7]

* * *

In 1 Colossians 2:20, Paul writes that it is not he who lives but
Christ who lives in him. Christ is in us: *that's* the hope of glory.

It wasn't "get saved, go to church, be a nice person, die, and go float on a cloud." It wasn't "do good things for the poor." It wasn't a list of dos and don'ts.

When Jesus stood up in the synagogue and read the words of the prophet Isaiah aloud into the incredulity of the crowd, He announced that these words had been fulfilled in their hearing, this is the Kingdom of God come and coming:

The Spirit of God, the Master, is on me
because God anointed me.
He sent me to preach good news to the poor,
heal the heartbroken,
Announce freedom to all captives,
pardon all prisoners.
God sent me to announce the year of His grace—
a celebration of God's destruction of our enemies—
and to comfort all who mourn,
To care for the needs of all who mourn in Zion,
give them bouquets of roses instead of ashes,
Messages of joy instead of news of doom,
a praising heart instead of a languid spirit.
Rename them "Oaks of Righteousness"
planted by God to display His glory.[8]

Now that's a life I want to join.

Dorothy Sayers wrote, "We have very efficiently pared the claws of the Lion of Judah, certified him 'meek and mild,' and recommended him as a fitting household pet for pale curates and pious old ladies. To those who knew him, however, he in no way suggests a milk-and-water person; they objected to him as a dangerous firebrand."[9]

I think that's because God is love.

* * *

Love is ferocious. Now the wrath of God is a great expression of God's love: it's the force that burns away everything that gets in the way of our full self, our clearest communion with God. It's a cure for the sickness of sin within us. God's love is meant to *heal* us; it is not a fire that rages *against* us. At the core of

God's love is the force that burns away everything that gets in the way of our full self.

redemption is a love story. The enemy is not us: we're caught in the war zone. It comes against the root of sin within us, saving us entirely.

So now when I think of that whole wrath-of-God thing, I think of it as a holy thing because it's born of love, it's directed at injustice and oppression, at anything that diminishes the *imago dei* in us.

I remember hearing once that Jesus came not only to save us and redeem us, but to show us what it means to be truly human. Because he was fully and completely human, He is our perfect example of the humanity we were meant to embody as we move through this life. And so we, as Christ followers, are truly human at last, awakened to the divine spark, the hands and feet and mouth and heart of Jesus. Eugene Peterson once wrote that Jesus was the one who would "say the big nouns: joy, glory, peace; and live the best verbs: love, forgive, save. Along with the swaddling clothes the words are washed of every soiling sentiment, scrubbed clean of all failed promises, then hung in the world's backyard dazzling white, billowing gospel." [10]

When I think of the Kingdom of God now, I think of those big nouns and best verbs, how we embody our prayers and hopes, how we move with God in the mission to rescue and restore and redeem, how we reflect Jesus in our loving and forgiving, embracing and welcoming, how we fling wide open the doors of the love we've found in humanity. Few things will reorient your life like discipleship: it's leaving behind a false humanity and entering into the truth of home at last, exiles returning.

* * *

Go for a drive just as the sun begins to sink away. Turn off the radio, and lean your head against the passenger side window and look up into the trees. Watch the light thread through the leaves, flicker, dance with the wind, moving like sunlight on an open lake.

The light is breaking through the trees; blink and you'll miss it but look, the light is here. It grows and takes over your senses. Even when you close your eyes, you see the light moving. You are bathed in the movement of light, but if it weren't for the trees, you wouldn't feel the waves.

We Christians, we have a saying about the Kingdom of God: it's now and it's not yet. We live in a tension. It's the tension of living our lives as Kingdom people, oriented around the life and teachings of our Jesus, a Christocentric people, in a world that is not yet redeemed. Of course the world is good—God made it good—and even though it has fallen, it will be restored.

We are balancing between the new upside-down Kingdom ways of our Jesus and the reality of our present age.

We are balancing between the new upside-down Kingdom ways of our Jesus and the reality of our present age. It means that even though all things are made new, they are still in the process of *being made* new. So we live in a fallen world and terrible things happen, but we live our lives as if the Kingdom has already come because it has, and yet, it is still coming.

I'll confess to you that I am often too quick to dismiss the "now" part of the Kingdom of God. It's easier to say, *"Marana-tha*, come, Lord Jesus," and wait for the sweet by-and-by to fix it all.

I think it's time for us to start leaning into the "now" part of the Kingdom of God a bit more.

I understand the Kingdom of God if I come at it from the corner of my eye instead of straight on. Like love, it defies definition and tidy resolutions and score sheets.

I am too focused on the not-yet part of the Kingdom. I focus my eyes and my life entirely on the despair or the brokenness, on the frustrations and injustices. I miss the beauty in the brokenness. I miss the Church living and breathing new life into death.

I missed the light because of the trees, instead of seeing that it is the movement and shadow of the trees that make the light even more brilliant. The trees aren't blocking the sunlight, they're making the light dance in our lives like dry bones rising up alive.

The Bride of Christ grows lovelier to me with each passing day; I keep finding our brothers and sisters in the strangest of places, quietly doing the work of the Kingdom, not because anybody "deserves" it or to appease some lesser deity but because *this is what we do. This is who we are.* This is the allegiance of the Kingdom, our calling is to live out our lives right now as if the Kingdom has already come, because it has. We have God's promises that all things will be made new, and so now: what do I see?

Beauty. Redemption. Miracles. Wholeness. Healing. Renewal. Friendship. Conversation. Prayer. Worship. Work. Music. Art. Justice. Jubilee. Mercy. Love. Sex. Aging.

I want to see the light and I want to see the trees. I want to learn to see them both, moving quickly, stirring with the wind of the Spirit.

I think the Kingdom is more poetry and life than it is definitions and boundaries. Go for a drive, go for a walk, go to work, look up, and fill your eyes with the Kingdom already come.

8

An Unexpected Legacy

ON THE ANCIENT PRACTICES

Part of my experience in sorting out my faith has been to remove and repurpose, to discard and to reclaim. But when it came to my heritage as a believer, there has also been discovery and newness, renewal in the ancient paths long forsaken. It felt like opening up an attic and finding treasures that were mine by birthright.

* * *

As a child, I liked to stand in the front row of our church. I kicked and stomped my small feet with abandon, causing the overhead projector to wobble precariously on the folding chair. We met in the community center on Sunday mornings to worship together and then on Friday nights at the leisure center to play floor hockey after our discipleship classes. We considered ourselves first-generation Christians, but really, we weren't. We just didn't know our heritage. We didn't know that others had come before us. The Bible spoke of a great cloud of witnesses, but we were unacquainted with them. We felt like lonely pilgrims instead of a vast company.

We were children of the renewal movement in Canada. To me, church wasn't stuffy or boring. Church had electric guitars and a keyboard. Preaching was tailored for us—the ones who didn't have a history of higher education and academics. We were middle-class and working-class.

Growing up as a charismatic evangelical, I had an understanding of spiritual formation that could be summed up in these steps:

1. Make sure you have your own personal quiet time reading the Word.
2. Spend time in prayer born from your heart and life.
3. Go to church on Sundays.

Simple and straightforward disciplines to practice, and life-changing for our family because we were so new to Scripture, to prayer, to church. And I still practice these disciplines today—even the church one (most of the time). But eventually I discovered the depth and width of Christian spiritual formation through the ages.

Even though I grew up in church, I didn't learn a hymn until my twenties. My pews were folding chairs. I had never heard of the Book of Common Prayer. My only exposure to liturgy and the Church calendar was through my love of literature, coming across references in dog-eared Jane Austen novels, for instance. Bingley took possession of Netherfield before Michaelmas. *What in the heck is Michaelmas?* I wondered. In the days before Google, I found myself flipping the pages of an encyclopedia at the local library. Oh, a feast day. End of September. Who knew, eh?

* * *

Here in Canada, we know our seasons by the light. In the summertime, the sun rises at 4:30 in the morning, and it's bright as day until long past when well-behaved tinies should be in their beds. In the winter, the sun begins to set at 3:30 in the afternoon and our nights stretch into cold morning stars. Every year, we go through the months of light and the months of dark, resolutely and steadily without argument. It's simply what happens here. This is how we live. We have learned to thrive in the darkness and to step into the light while it's ours to enjoy. In my faith, I see the same cycles: there are seasons of darkness and rest in the secret places and cold renewal punctuated only by the moon and the stars; and then there are seasons of bright light and celebration and long days of warmth. I'm enough of a mystic to believe that our place informs our theology, and so as we travel around the sun, I have found God as much in the early nights as in the long days.

> *I'm enough of a mystic to believe that our place informs our theology.*

I had no language or theology for it, but even as a child, I knew that the Holy Spirit was there in the sadness and quiet and fallow seasons that sometimes came to me. In fact, God more often met me there in the valley of the shadow than in my mountain-top moments.

My faith tradition is what Barbara Brown Taylor would call "the solar Christians."[1] Our faith and our answers exist primarily in the narrative of victory, simplicity, and certainty—in the bright light of day. But there has always been a lunar soul within me—I think there is in most of us—and in my tradition, our sadness, our loss, even our loneliness, is often unacknowledged.

When I moved to the United States in the nineties for university, I was dazzled by all the Christians and their certainty, their cultural power. For a kid who grew up going to church in living rooms and leisure centers, these massive megachurches were quite a thrill. For instance, I remember standing in a gigantic stadium on a regular Sunday morning, thousands of people surrounding me. I felt alive and bright as the sun—every cell thrumming with passion and connection. I had no idea there were other ways to engage with God, so I tried harder. Light is certainty; you move more cautiously in the darkness.

But a few years later, I was at the point where I wanted to skip church every Sunday. I had just lost another baby before birth. I felt that I couldn't go to church because there was no room for my grief or my questions or my doubt there. In a tradition that was filled with victory and the shiny, happy joy of properly answered prayers and neat equations, I felt like I didn't belong. I was lamenting,

I felt that I couldn't go to church because there was no room for my grief or my questions there.

questioning, I was grieving, I was doubting everything I thought I knew about God and myself and Church. Where else could I go from here but to the wilderness? The wilderness was so real to me, it felt like a real place: there I met God.

And as often happens with grief, this melancholy of mine began to include more than just my own experiences. When your heart breaks, anyone or anything can tumble in. Part of me thinks this is the right thing anyway: that's probably where we all belong, being carried along in each other's tender hearts. Those cracks in my heart helped me awaken to the real world thumping along beside our lovely building campaigns and programs with parking attendants and light shows to keep things bright in the artificial room.

This is why I began to reorient my life around the only one who made sense to my broken heart: Jesus. He was the only one I knew who embodied it all, who welcomed it all, experienced it all without pretense. He understood my light and my dark, my hope and my despair; He experienced my suffering. He was beauty and He was the way, the truth, and the life. In my despair, I turned to the crucified Lamb of God, the whole Jesus, wild and untamed and countercultural instead of my carefully curated version of Him.

* * *

Perhaps it's because I'm writing this as our fourth wee baby has just arrived earthside, but most of my metaphors these days find their way to my experiences with giving birth. I have learned now that physiologically and biologically, and even spiritually, women often crave darkness and quiet during birth. We are not as removed from our fellow creatures as our medicalization of birth would have us believe. I know that everyone has a very different story and sensibility when it comes to giving birth, so this is only mine.

Even when I delivered my eldest in a more modern way, my body cried out for silence and darkness. I couldn't do the work of birth with the bright lights or artificial cheerfulness of strangers. It stalled me; it made the pain more intense; it made me afraid at a subconscious level beyond my reason. But when

I delivered at my own home, I saw the difference when I could indulge what my body and spirit craved at a place beyond education and logic and reason. Birth has been the most human and most sacred act of my life so far.

For new life to come forth, I need quiet and darkness. I need fewer people—only trusted and quiet people—and fewer interruptions. I need to focus and to enter fully into what my body is doing. There is a direct connection between tension and fear and our inability to lean into the pain. Leaning into the pain, becoming one with the pain of labor and welcoming it without judgment, is solitary work, requiring my full concentration. The fewer people, the less light, the less interference, the better it goes for me.

When I was in labor with my second baby, my husband was the one who called my attention to this. It was just us two for most of my labor, but eventually I asked him to stop talking, to just be present with me but not to speak, and he said, "Now we're close to the end." I almost laughed at him—how could he possibly know? But he knew that this was my indicator: when I want presence but silence, he said, when I go very deeply inward, we are near birth. And he was right— this was my point of transition to the final stages. Joseph was born very shortly after that.

I know now that the Spirit is trying to birth something in my life when I find myself craving silence and darkness.

I know now that the Spirit is trying to birth something in my life when I find myself craving silence and darkness, when I find myself editing my circle down to just the trusted few whom I know will midwife me through this birth. It's nothing to fear; it's the time of transition.

* * *

I found myself wandering into the Anglican Church many years ago. I still have no idea why I did this. I was craving an encounter with the Spirit, but my grief had erected too great a wall between me and my tradition. I couldn't seem to bring myself to go to the stadium-style church with light shows and happy-clappy choruses. I found myself craving a God who would meet me in lament and silence and darkness. When I spotted a tiny stone church downtown near my work, shadowed with live oak trees, I felt drawn to it.

I randomly pulled in, and it happened to be an Ash Wednesday service. I sat in the back row to listen, and I thought, *I have no idea what is happening right now.* It was confusing and weird to me, but there in the liturgy of Ash Wednesday, as we prayed and read and worshipped through the admission of our sin, I released a breath I didn't know I had been holding.

Finally. Finally someone was acknowledging the shadows, the grief, the repentance, the sometimes inescapable sorrow of our existence.

I found myself heading up the aisle with the congregation to have some guy in a robe draw a cross on my forehead out of ashes. Now I would say that I was compelled by the Spirit to receive the imposition of the ashes, because when the priest touched my forehead and said the words, "Remember you are dust and to dust you shall return," it seemed as if the disconnected joint in my spirit between the solar and the lunar was popped back into its right place. We prayed through the Psalms, we listened to the challenges of prophetic Isaiah, we read the Gospels, we prayed and confessed our way corporately through a litany of repentance:

Most holy and merciful Father: We confess to you and
to one another, and to the whole communion of saints
in heaven and on earth, that we have sinned by our own
fault in thought, word, and deed; by what we have done,
and by what we have left undone.[2]

* * *

But make no mistake: I wasn't longing for "more candles" or a
cool new experience to chase.

I was craving Jesus. Desperately.

Not seven steps to a better life, not practical how-to stuff for
the week ahead, not more sermons about "what women really
want." I certainly wasn't longing for vestments and hierarchy,
smells or bells: I was longing for Jesus. I wanted to be with
people who loved Him too. I longed to remember Him, to com-
mune with Him, to sit in His dust in the dark and in the light,
and to learn, as Jesus offered in Matthew 11:28–30, how to live
freely and lightly in the unforced rhythm of grace.

Jesus.

I simply wanted Jesus, and since I couldn't seem to part
the weeds in my own tradition to find His face (that, most as-
suredly, was because of my own baggage), I began to walk in
the well-worn paths that the pilgrims before me had carved out.
The Holy Spirit met me there, in a blend between my own past
and the ancient heritage of my faith, helping me find a way to
the future, to my born-again-all-over-again self.

When I couldn't find my way through the clutter of praise
and worship, I found Jesus in the silence and in the liturgy.
When I couldn't go into a megachurch, I could sneak into a
small chapel and light a candle. When I had no words to pray,
the Book of Common Prayer gave me back the gift of prayer.

When I couldn't sing along with certainty, I could hold a hymn book and simply listen, let the voices of others carry me. When I was consumed with my own life, blinders on, the liturgy reoriented me to the real story—to redemption, justice, and confession and to worship and community. I learned to orient worship around Christ and the Spirit and the Father.

And just like the grief stained everything, the hope and the rebirth—my Jesus—brought that renewal and the new narrative of wholeness to my life.

* * *

For me, the ancient practices of the Church were new ground.

Which is utterly adorable, I know. I felt like a brand-new believer instead of what I actually was: a woman who by then had gone to church for twenty years. I sat through liturgies I didn't understand, picked up the wrong books, stood when I should have remained seated. The code had to be cracked: for instance, "passing the peace" meant shaking hands and saying "peace be with you" to the people who sat near me.

Instead of a Hallmark calendar shaping the conversation of the Church (which was my own tradition), moving us from Valentine's Day to Mother's Day to the national holidays, the people of God through the ages have followed their own rhythm, in the world but not of it. When I began to follow the liturgical calendar, I moved outside my own pet passages and selective reading of Scripture to embrace the whole story with Christ at the center of everything.

When I began to follow the liturgical calendar, I began to embrace the whole story with Christ at the center of everything.

* * *

At the beginning of my journey into the ancient practices, I was filled with grief for my own small concerns, yes, but also for the world. I had run out of words. And faith. I was grieving in a personal and spiritual way. I had lost another child before birth, and my house was empty. And I was grieving on a global scale too: the Iraq War was beginning, my heart was being broken for the poor and the oppressed and the marginalized of our society—particularly our women—and I was silent in the face of it.

I couldn't pray in the overcomer, faith-filled victory way that had become part of my life. The way that I knew how to pray felt empty at best, at worst a futile effort at wresting control.

Silence was akin to prayer for me for a long time. I simply moved through my life with silence in my spirit, waiting on God. I couldn't pray, but the part of me that had once prayed was waiting. Simply waiting.

And then I discovered praying the hours. I heard about it in a book, which is how I seem to discover most things. I was reading Kathleen Norris's *Amazing Grace: A Vocabulary of Faith*,[3] and she was writing about her time with Benedictine monks and praying the hours, and my thumbs pricked. *What was this?*

That pricking, I believe now, was the Holy Spirit. At the right time, I was given this legacy. So I began to investigate it. When I picked up my first copy of the Book of Common Prayer, I found the tiny maroon book horribly confusing, like a foreign language. Then I realized that Phyllis Tickle had a series of books for prayer called *The Divine Hours*,[4] which basically organized those prayers and explained them for people like me—the toddling charismatics stumbling along the Canterbury Trail.

That was my beginning point. And for ten years now, I've prayed the hours. I began to pray the hours out of desperation because I had forgotten how to pray. I simply couldn't pray anymore. Sometimes I pray the hours with more regularity than other times, but they've been the constant in my life. Praying the hours was like a new time zone, a new way to structure and move through my day with prayer as the scaffolding.

I think I draw as much comfort from the knowledge that I am not alone as I pray, as I do from the words and discipline itself.

* * *

When I "discovered" the liturgy, it wasn't as a stranger. It was as a reminder, a legacy. This isn't a new thing to us; this is who we are as a church and as a people. It's not observance, it's participation. It's work. It's dialogue.

When I began to pray the hours, I remembered how to pray. It wasn't just about discipline or quiet time, as we call it. It was about making my story bigger than myself. It was about getting me out of the center spot in my life and reorienting my heart—my spirit, my mind, my words, and even my time—to Jesus Christ. And I needed to be reminded of that bigger story.

When I began to pray the hours, I remembered how to pray.

* * *

I've learned to light my candles for the days when life is a little unsatisfying. I light a small votive in my house after I listen to a friend on the phone, after I meet with another friend from church, after I walk out of the doctor's office with another prescription for antibiotics for a strep throat in the tinies, after I read the news, after I am hurt, after the dissatisfaction and the longing for God to come near to us rises up in me like an altar begging for fire to descend.

I light the candle in the middle of the house and every time I see it, I breathe out the names and their places, the people I'm carrying for that day.

It's one of the habits of my heart: I light the candle in the middle of the house and every time I see it, I breathe out the names and their places, the people I'm carrying for that day.

This week alone, I have listened to stories of bitterness and unforgiveness, adoption struggles, death and sickness, betrayal and addictions, loss and grief, sleepless nights with sick children, and longings unfulfilled in the hearts and lives of people I love. And there are more questions than answers. Among us, there is sorrow. And then there is the world around us: the hungry bellies, the dirty water, the vicious war, the waiting and lonely children silent behind chain-link fences in refugee camps, the women caught in sex trafficking, our culture's exploitative violence masquerading as entertainment, and . . . Lord, have mercy.

When I tell a friend I will pray for her, the candle on my mantle reminds me to pray often, holding my friend up to our Jesus with faith. And I still pray in tongues, yes, I do. And I pray in beautiful obscurity as I move through my day and do laundry or cook or knit or clean and write. I am still me and I pray like me. I'm also learning to embody my prayer—to become the answers.

* * *

I remember hearing about spiritual disciplines with the metaphor of parts of a sailboat from John Ortberg.[5] Spiritual disciplines like praying the hours or *lectio divina* and Bible reading, or even tithing or celebration or silence or fasting—they're like a sailboat. You have to prepare. You have to set up your boat well, you must raise the sail, and then you must maintain the tools and materials. Over the years, you learn best practices from others more expert than yourself. And even with all that knowledge, ultimately, it's the wind that moves the boat. In our metaphor, the Holy Spirit breathes on the boat and makes it move. But by practicing these things, we put ourselves in a posture of readiness. So when the Spirit comes into our life—whether it's through our grief or our joy, our hope or our sadness, our personal disciplines or our communal prayers—we are ready to move with God.

> *By practicing these things, we put ourselves in a posture of readiness. So when the Spirit comes into our life, we are ready to move with God.*

* * *

On the Christian calendar it was Trinity Sunday, but it was also Father's Day. Since we have had our fill of Father's Day observance, we decided to eschew the usual, and we went to a liturgical church in town. This small church had been dying for years; it was filled with white hair and traditions. We sat in the back row with our pew-full of children to shush. We stood and sat, we kneeled. By then, I knew the words. I'd cracked the code. We spoke the liturgy, we prayed the prayers of the day. The preaching was excellent. The service was perfectly ordered. The leaders wore vestments, candles were lit, the singing was atrocious, but the prayers were beautiful. It was completely different from our usual Sunday morning experience, so the tinies were alternately fascinated and bored.

And when we left, I felt rather wistful and out of place still. We didn't belong there.

I haven't been able to leave my own mother church. I still find myself most at home in the school gym with the cho-ruses and the clamor, with the unscripted moments and our own version of liturgy. I missed the noise, I missed our music, I

I haven't been able to leave my own mother church.

missed the diversity, I missed the simplicity and lack of affectation. I missed the low-church sensibility close to the dirt. I have tried to leave, for one reason or another, but I keep coming home.

My life has been enriched by the treasure of ancient practices, but now I feel as if I fit nowhere. I'm liturgical but I'm also happy-clappy, I'm ancient practices and new expressions, I'm school gymnasiums and cathedrals, I'm liturgy and the renewal of the Spirit, I'm the Church calendar and the freedom to pray in tongues. I find God in both of those places and everywhere between, so in the end, I've turned out to need us all, the whole family of God.

Every night at bedtime, we pray the Lord's Prayer with our tinies—the old King James version, in fact. That was the version I memorized, complete with the "thy" and "thou" affectations, and so it's the version I know to pray when I'm tired at the end of the day. When we stood for the Lord's Prayer at this very different church with a very different crowd where we felt so terribly out of place because of our age and our season of life and our personal church his-

tory, their little faces lit up when *In the end, I've turned out* they realized that they knew the *to need us all, the whole* words. The tinies prayed loud and *family of God.* proud—little charismatics—along

with this aging and sparsely populated tiny church, and it felt for a moment like we were all together still.

But we never went back. I know when I'm beat. I feel too homesick in the cathedrals and chapels. I still need folding chairs and flags.

Perhaps it makes sense then that those practices have only grounded me further into my own tradition. Liturgy and tradition enriched my life, but they haven't changed my place of belonging. But even so, I miss the traditions and the language of the calendar and the liturgy almost every Sunday of my life.

* * *

Nellie left me a few teacups, and I keep them out on display. They are among my dearest possessions. Delicate but within budget, each one is different, nary a match among the five of them. These teacups have tea stains inside from fifty years of filling, and there are a few hairline cracks, so I don't dare use three of them. I do use the other two quite often; I think of her each time that I do. Nellie knew I loved them both for her sake and for their own sake. I also have a lovely ornate teacup from Buckingham Palace. I've never been there, mind you, but my parents went to London once upon a time and they bought it for me. I love to look at it—intricate scrollwork, a wide base, perfectly made. Somehow it makes me glad to see the pristine alongside the humble, to see the ways that the old and the new, the everyday and the special occasion, eventually belong to-gether.

* * *

Our young adults group at church has a monthly get-together they call Soup and the Spirit. It's their time to eat together and pray and study. They asked me to come one Sunday afternoon and tell them about Lent. We ate lentil stew and hunks of bread, we prayed in tongues together, we laid hands on the suffering as we prayed, we sang songs to the single guitar, then I read the prayers and the Scriptures, and I taught about Church history and the purpose of Lent. They listened and then we talked about how this practice can be spirit-breathed among us even today. It was a mosaic of all the things I love best about all of us, and it was beautiful.

Somehow it makes me glad to see the ways that the old and the new eventually belong together.

I got my start in the small, organic faith churches of west-ern Canada, and it was good, but I needed the kindness of the conservative Southern Baptist pastors' wives I discovered in my early twenties, and I needed the Mennonites to teach me about pacifism and thrift, and I needed the megachurch's passion and anonymity, and I needed the intense studying of newly re-formed friends, and I needed the mysticism of my charismatic roots, and I needed the desert *abbas* and *ammas*.

I needed *lectio divina*, a labyrinth, liturgy, and the Jesus Prayer, I needed my Bible, and I needed the Book of Common Prayer. I needed the established theologians and poets and the up-and-coming bold bloggers, I needed the emerging church, and now I need my little community Vineyard. I need happy-clappy Jesus music, and I need the old hymns I sing into the cavern of the bathtub while I wash these small souls in my care, and I need Mumford & Sons too. I needed my husband's seminary textbooks and discussions, and I needed big hairy worship anthems in stadiums with light shows, and then, when I didn't, I needed empty cathedrals, pubs, the Eucharist every week, open fields, and church outside the lines, and I need it all, still, always. I hold it all inside.

Like a lot of us these days, I defy the easy categories for sorting. I'm an Anglican-influenced charismatic, postevangelical with a strong pull toward Anabaptist theology. Say that three times fast. I speak in tongues and I pray the hours. I dance and clap at church, but I also sit in silence and meditation. I place my hands on people when I pray for them, and I light candles. I follow the Church calendar observing Lent and Pentecost, Advent and ordinary time, but I worship in community with believers who do not—and likely never will—and I belong there. Perhaps I'm a bit greedy. I don't want to choose between them. I don't want to choose between the people who first showed me Jesus and the people who made sure I got to hold on to Jesus and the ones who keep me even now.

Wild Goose

ON FAITH, THE SPIRIT, SIGNS, AND WONDERS

Our family came to Jesus through signs and wonders. This is my legacy. Brennan Manning writes, "A mystic is a person whose life is ruled by thirst."[1] I am still thirsty.

As a young man, my father suffered with fear and anxiety. Medications didn't work. Alternative therapies didn't work. Nothing relieved him from the grip of anxiety that strangled his life. He developed painful stomach ulcers and began to withdraw more and more from public life. He couldn't go to a company dinner without agony, so he simply stopped going. He became withdrawn and ill, losing weight and overcome with despair at the thought of an entire lifetime filled not only with the fear but the managing of the fear.

When my mother had her own supernatural experience with the Lord, thanks to that children's record from our fourteen-year-old babysitter (you can't make this stuff up), he went along with her to church, even though he was a to-the-bone skeptic and battled anxiety about the whole experience. My father is western Canadian to the core—practical, hardworking, a bit distrustful of "the establishment" or the elite. But it was at this

Presbyterian church that he first heard that God could heal people. The reverend dared my father to believe God could heal him. And sure enough, my father took the dare. He went home and prayed for the first time in his recollection. He told God that he wasn't sure about the whole church thing and he wasn't sure about the whole God thing, but if He was real, to prove it and heal him. Never mind your formulas and your "right ways to pray": God met him there in the living room right then, swept into his life with power, and healed him, from the chemical imbalances in his brain to his ulcers to the visceral grip of fear in his heart. He has been healed ever since.

The priest dared my father to believe God could heal him. And sure enough, my father took the dare.

And so I grew up believing God would break through time and space, through the laws of nature and physical law, for all of us.

We prayed for and about everything—healing from headaches, good parking spots at the mall (a good parking spot is a big deal when it is minus thirty degrees outside), for our friends or family members to become Christians, for good sleep, for a raise, for wisdom. We prayed guilelessly and easily, like children, convinced that the safest place was in our Father's presence. We felt no shame for standing with our hands outstretched.

* * *

When you come of age as I did, in a world where the mysteries of our faith are spoken of with such certainty of control, the experience often leaves you with more questions than answers. And yet somehow I find I've become more charismatic the older

I've gotten. My journey brought me back again. The more I
wrestle and refine and reform, the more I lean on that strain of
mysticism, that wild unearthly note of wind and fire, the metaphors of the river and the dove. I'm thirsty for the in-breaking
of the Spirit. I want the incarnation and Emmanuel, I want
tongues of fire and words of wisdom, I want miracles and heal-
ings, I yearn for visions and dreams.

The more I study and dissect and critically discuss my experiences and my beliefs, the more deeply convinced I have
become of God's breaking-through power and of the need for
the wild goose of the Holy Spirit soaring among us, beautiful
and ordinary, in this present age.

* * *

When I was very young, I was given the gift of speaking in
tongues.

On Friday nights, our little church of misfits would meet at
the Regina Leisure Center to play floor hockey after a lively
Bible study. The adults would hunch over notebooks, scrib-
bling furiously as their leader taught Bible stories and prin-
ciples for life, but we kids were in a separate room for our
age-appropriate Bible study. A middle-aged lady taught our
class, and one winter night, she spoke to us of a special prayer
language, a gift from heaven. I don't really remember much of
what she said, but I remember the weight of her warm hand on
my small head, her quiet voice praying so only I could hear,
asking Jesus for "a special language that is just between her
own heart and you, Jesus." I trusted this woman completely:
she loved Jesus, and I could feel that in her warmth. Jesus was
the axis for my world, everything I knew and loved about life
turned on Him, and at that moment, my childish voice began to

speak out in a whisper. It sounded odd but somehow homey to my heart, this murmuring language rolled against the back of my front teeth, and I felt joy, joy, joy down in my heart.

But ever since that day, I've wrestled with the gift of tongues as both the outsider and the insider.

When I grew up, I learned that speaking in tongues is considered a fringe aspect of Christianity. Not only did hardly anyone speak in tongues, but many Christians thought it was fake, manipulative. It was wrong to pursue it, to want it. People made fun of it, babbling, *"Shundai-shundai-shoulda-bought-a-Hyundai"* and I would laugh along nervously.

> *I've wrestled with the gift of tongues as both the outsider and the insider.*

And many were certain that speaking in other languages didn't even exist anymore, scaring me a bit with the thump of a closed-door Bible. No more tongues, they told me, it simply isn't for today. So then I wondered if they were right: was I emotionally manipulated that day? Am I just faking it? Is it really necessary to me, and what does it mean? How does this work in public or in private? I felt ostracized, like I had to keep this gift quiet and hidden for a long time.

Then, as an insider to this gift, I cringed at loud prayer meetings where people wildly hollered consonants and vowels, never a thought to order or interpretations. The hours of sweaty church services with "speaking in tongues" as part of the circus also included falling out, wild laughter, and my own deep sense of discomfort.

When people preached about it or talked about it, they acted like *we* had it figured out, and every one else was somehow less spiritual. The work of the Spirit was linked to salvation; those who hadn't experienced it *might* be saved, but this "second baptism" was the real determiner of who was *in* and who was *out*.

We attached the label "spirit-filled" to ourselves, implying that we owned the Holy Spirit, and the rest of you, well, you weren't living in the fullness that we were.

It confused me because I knew that the work of the Spirit is never one of division and pride. And I saw the hurt of friends who deeply loved the Lord and yet were never given the gift of tongues themselves but were made to feel as if they lacked faith. I also knew that the work and fruit of the Spirit was oftentimes growing and thriving more obviously in the lives of those we deemed "not spirit-filled." Some of the best, most joyful, most faithful Christians I knew did not speak in tongues. So clearly, we were wrong a lot of the time. And we hurt a lot of people with our exclusivity.

Part of my own journey has been to finally admit and embrace that I am a bit of a mystic. I'm thirsty for the Spirit. Speaking in tongues is my first language when words fail—which, in this life, happens often. While I labored in our home to give birth to another tiny, barely-there baby that we would not hold in this life, my burning tears were tasted by a mouth that only spoke tongues for those long hours, my heart somehow groaning along with my body, and my grief and worship and trust joined together. And then when I labored to bring the tinies we do hold earthside, again, in the ecstasy, it was my gift, the baptism of motherhood and pain somehow coming alongside in a hallelujah, and I knew that every word I whispered was an "Oh, *thank you*" in every language of the world.

And somehow this speaking wends its way into my most joyful moments, my quiet and contemplative ones, my questions and my wonderings, my anger and my sadness. Tongues is where I turn when my heart is wrung out by injustice and evil and suffering. Sometimes I have an active interpretation, sometimes it leads me to Scripture, and other times it's just a gift, syllables of peace for the saving of my own soul. Rarely a day goes by that I am not drawn to the practice of this gift.

Yet I hold that gift while I hold the sorrow for the hurt and abuses, the implied exclusivity, the bad theology, and the sometimes even worse subculture around charismatic gifts. That's not the work of the Spirit, I know that much.

The work of the believer is to speak first the life of the Spirit, apples of gold and wisdom, dripping silver and emeralds of life, that fill us with love, joy, peace, patience, kindness, goodness, faithfulness, gentleness, and self-control. Because, "if I speak with the tongues of men and of angels, but do not have love, I have become a noisy gong or a clanging cymbal. And if I have the gift of prophecy, and know all mysteries and all knowledge; and if I have all faith, so as to remove mountains, but do not have love, I am nothing. . . . But now abide faith, hope, love, these three; but the greatest of these is love."[2] Against such things, even the most stout cessationist or wild charismatic knows, there is no law, so let Love be my first language, my mother tongue, whether it's communicated in English or a thousand tongues for only angels to hear.

* * *

I know that some people are discouraged by the lack of unity among Christians in the world. We point to the three main branches of Christianity—Eastern Orthodox, Roman Catholic, and Protestant—and their own convoluted histories with sadness, as an example of the ways that the Church universal is fragmented and divided. Protestant denominations number around forty-one thousand.[3]

But I sort of like how we're spread all over the place and how we each have our own way of worshipping or understanding God while still being part of the same family. I think it's one of the beauties of Christianity. I see the different kinds of Christians not as exclusively a lack of unity, but as affirmations of our diversity—the ways that God has reached us and spoken to us, the ways that God works with us and in us, with unique beauty. For the one who craves logic, there is a stream for you. For the one who craves liturgy and tradition, there is a stream for you.

The ways I need redemption and community may be different from yours. But we need each

> *I like how we're spread all over the place and how we each have our own way of worshipping or understanding God while still being part of the same family.*

other, and we need to learn from each stream, because our stories don't happen alone; our roots are all tangled together. The logical ones need the mystics, the mystics need the traditionalists, the liturgists need the new song, the experiential need the *sola scriptura* crowd. The Church has crept and stumbled, sailed and spun around the world, and yet, we are a family tree still. Sure, a few branches would love to cut themselves off from the rest of us, but we're still connected, our histories are entwined. I have found my home in one branch, but I keep visiting the homes of the rest of my family to learn and to connect, to swap stories before heading back to my own place.

As a movement, we look back to Pentecost, a story that opens the book of Acts and launches this ragtag group into becoming

18

160 Out of Sorts

the early church. Jesus' last promise before His ascension is an important one: "But you will receive power when the Holy Spirit comes upon you. And you will be my witnesses, telling people about me everywhere—in Jerusalem, throughout Judea, in Samaria, and to the ends of the earth."[4] After that, 120 disciples, including Mary the Mother of Jesus, were gathered in an upper room. They had been meeting together for prayer when, as Scripture says, the Holy Spirit came upon them.

The Holy Spirit came upon them.

Don't you love that phrase? It gives me chills to read what happened next: "Suddenly, there was a sound from heaven like the roaring of a mighty windstorm, and it filled the house where they were sitting. Then, what looked like flames or tongues of fire appeared and settled on each of them. And everyone present was filled with the Holy Spirit and began speaking in other languages, as the Holy Spirit gave them this ability."[5]

Their gathering caught the eye of everyone who was in town for the feast. People thought they were drunk and jeered at them. But others realized that they weren't simply jabbering but rather that they were speaking in other languages—an unimaginable feat for a group of uneducated Galileans. Then Peter stood up and preached a powerful sermon, bringing three thousand souls to Christ that day. The power of the Spirit was the great evangelist. The second chapter of Acts ends with this image of the early church, an image that apparently didn't last but still stands as the beacon of light for Christian community:

All the believers devoted themselves to the apostles' teaching, and to fellowship, and to sharing in meals (including the Lord's Supper), and to prayer. A deep sense of awe came over them all, and the apostles performed many miraculous signs and wonders. And all the believers met together in one place and shared everything they had. They sold their property and possessions and shared the money with those in need. They worshiped together at the Temple each day, met in homes for the Lord's Supper, and shared their meals with great joy and generosity—all the while praising God and enjoying the goodwill of all the people. And each day the Lord added to their fellowship those who were being saved.[6]

I don't think it's possible to overstate how much that story permeates the Pentecostal/charismatic movements. The power of the Holy Spirit as recorded through the early church is one of the great challenges and invitations for us today. The early church actively expected and anticipated the interference and leading of the Spirit; it expected mighty acts of God, and it expected to be led. The early church demonstrated a devotion to and dependence on the Spirit. We yearned for that deep sense of awe, for the miraculous signs and wonders. We

The power of the Holy Spirit as recorded through the early church is one of the great challenges and invitations for us today.

longed for worship and community, joy and generosity. And we longed for others to experience the same, longed to see many added to our number.

Though differences and splinters have arisen within the charismatic movement over the years, for the most part, the movement has been refined and reformed beautifully. For every excess, there has been a return to balance. For every misstep, there has been a correction. Theological schools were created, accountability structures put in place, and leaders, biblical

scholars, and teachers began to arise as the years went by—
all helping to develop the spiritual formation necessary for the
movements to grow in a healthy way. The excess and extreme
wings of our movement were still there, much as they are in
every denomination or movement, but I've even tried to appre-
ciate them for their very excess. They keep us reforming, keep
us wondering and awake. Of course most of the time, they also
frustrate me to no end.

Out of all the movements of Christianity, our tribe of Pente-
costalism or charismatic Christians is still the fastest growing
in the world. As Harvard theologian Harvey Cox says, Pente-
costalism is "reshaping religion in the 21st century."[7] People
who moan and groan about the waning influence of the Church
have forgotten the global story.

* * *

We charismatics pointed often to the life and ministry of Jesus
Himself. We looked to His words in John 5:19: "I tell you the
truth, the Son can do nothing by Himself. He does only what
He sees the Father doing. Whatever the Father does, the Son
also does." Jesus had just healed a lame man when He made
the claim to be the Son of God. As Jack Deere wrote in *Surprised by the Power of the Spirit*, "The miraculous ministry
of Jesus was absolutely dependent on His intimacy with His
Father. Likewise, the ministry of the apostles was absolutely
dependent on their intimacy with Jesus, for without Him they
could do nothing (John 15:5). Therefore, the loss of intimacy
means the loss of power for ministry."[8]

Perhaps that is why I grew up with such an intimate view of
Jesus, why we talked so easily of Jesus in our churches, why He
was the focus of our worship and adoration. We longed for that

intimacy because we believed it was key to the Holy Spirit's movement in our lives.

I think the movement lost me when it began to seek the signs and the wonders first, instead of Jesus. "It is possible to put almost any good thing above Jesus Christ without realizing what we are doing. We can put the Bible and its commandments above the Lord. We can put the spiritual gifts and even various kinds of worship above the Lord. We can put various forms of ministry—witnessing, caring for the poor, praying for the sick—above the Lord. It is possible to be seduced by all of these things," laments Deere.[9]

> *I think the movement lost me when it began to seek the signs and the wonders first, instead of Jesus.*

* * *

My early experiences within my tradition now seem pure-hearted. Yes, there was what Gordon Fee called some "over-realized eschatology."[10] Yes, there was literalism and pick-and-choose Bible reading. Yes, there was some name-it-and-claim-it, blab-it-and-grab-it theology and a simple narrowness exclusive to our context without an eye on the larger picture of God's redemption or heart for justice. But it had a purity to it, a smallness, an earnestness, and sincerity.

It was real to me.

God met us there and our hearts would always be entangled with the Spirit. It was a good way to come to faith, a good way to grow up. Right from the start, I took in the truth that God is good. God is good. God can be trusted, God loves, we are loved, and God's heart is ever and always for us. God is the origin of all goodness and wholeness. And our lives are meant to demonstrate or prophesy to that goodness.

But I remember something shifting in the early nineties. Perhaps that's my own memory and narrowness of experience, but the Toronto Blessing, which broke out in 1994, changed everything for the movement—and my place in it. Like many churches around North America, we were fascinated with the awakening in Toronto and longed for revival to spread out here to the West. The roots of the revival were in South America, and it brought Canadian churches and American preachers together. All across the continent, perhaps the world, Pentecostals, charismatics, and neo-charismatics would meet together for hours and hours to sing the same songs, say the same words, pray the same prayers, beg for the same manifestations and miracles.

This new movement included physical healing and a renewed emphasis on experiencing God's life-transforming love, but it quickly began to include "falling out" or "being slain in the Spirit." People would line up at the altar for prayer, and the leaders would put their hands on people's hands or shoulders and pray. Ushers stood behind each person, because the person seeking prayer would inevitably "fall out"—collapse to the floor for a time of communion with the Spirit—and the ushers were there to make sure no one fell too hard. Then someone would step forward to gracefully drape your lower body with a prayer cloth so that your dignity remained intact, and there you would lie. Slayed. In the Spirit. *Slain in the spirit.*

People would eventually rise again of their own volition— some within minutes, others after hours—to tell stories of how the Spirit had ministered to them, healed them, revealed visions or dreams to them, encouraged them, or set them free. Meanwhile, the music would play and people in their chairs would lift their hands or dance or sink to their knees in worship.

I went forward for prayer one night, probably the last time I did so for nearly twenty years. I stood in the lineup, longing for a touch of the Spirit, like so many around me. Someone came along and began to pray loudly for me, laying hands on my head and my shoulders. Most of what that person "prophesied" wasn't true at all. They claimed to be hearing from God, but I was growing more and more uncomfortable. I stood my ground. But the person praying *pushed* me backward into the waiting arms of an usher, who laid me down. A cloth was draped over my legs. And I was left on the floor in disbelief: the anointing had been faked, and people were shouting hallelujah over the whole thing.

Then came the focus on the joy of the Lord, and the congregations would erupt in "holy laughter"—laughter that spread and continued throughout the room, people reporting great happiness or joy in their hearts. But there were others who acted as if they were vomiting and claimed that it was because the Spirit had come upon them, causing them to "vomit" their unforgiveness or sin, to cast it off from themselves with immediacy. Then some began to roar like lions or bark like dogs; others claimed that God was giving them money, raining down gold from the ceiling or replacing their natural teeth with gold teeth as a manifestation of His eternal riches. There were exorcisms, dabblings in demonology, harsh prayers with physical assaults to "cast out" devils.

And yet when I talk about those days, when I remember them, I also remember this: some of it was real. I have no doubt of that. What is that elusive line between our flesh and our spirit leading? I don't know. Because for everyone like me who was pushed to the ground, who was grieved and disturbed

For everyone like me who was manipulated and pushed to the ground, there was someone who was healed, someone who was saved.

by the displays, there was someone who was healed, someone who was set free, someone who was saved.

Sometimes. Maybe. Who knows.

* * *

Anytime I want to get angry with people for making fun of us charismatics or talking about us in stereotypes and caricatures, I remember these days, and then I figure we probably deserve both the mockery and the criticism. Perhaps the real miracle from that awakening is that any of us are still Christians. When Brian and I get swapping stories of the craziest and weirdest and most abusive stuff we have seen in church, committed in the name of the Spirit, we marvel that any of us stuck around this whole Jesus thing. If the sum of my experiences with the charismatic movement were a few weird years in the nineties, I'd have cashed in long ago. But I emerged relatively unscathed except for a healthy dose of skepticism. For those who were more seriously abused or manipulated, the cost was much higher. God have mercy.

My friend Kelley calls herself a careful charismatic. I like that phrase and have adopted it as my own. She writes of the progression from being a clumsy charismatic to a careful one in this way:

My reading turned to the prophets of old—Isaiah, Amos, Micah. Their signs and wonders felt like an afterthought compared to their incessant concern for the vulnerable within the community. These men spoke of neighborhood restoration, rivers of justice, and my favorite, melting swords and fashioning plowshares. They called out economic exploitation, violence, and tribalism that di-

vided. The Spirit energized them to emancipate people
from real debt, real slavery, real peril. These prophetic
voices changed what I wanted. I no longer wanted to be
on the superhighway of information or be a street fighter.
I wanted to see people set free from the underside of
empires and economies so they could live a viable and
vibrant life. And, like any prophet worth her salt, they
scrubbed down my own pretense. In a season that was
quite quiet and unremarkable, the Spirit recalibrated
me. Nothing was lost, but everything was transformed.
My language shifted. Gone were my careless words, my
overfamiliarity with the divine and casual talk of how the
Spirit was at work here or there. I held my tongue more.
I watched. I listened. My hunger for justice deepened. I
saw the Spirit at work in places I'd missed before, and
it broke me and freed me at the same time. I still speak
in tongues. My hand still trembles slightly when I pray.
I've witnessed God heal a little girl of full-blown AIDS
and take a community of families into food security for
the first time in their lives. I believe the Spirit is alive
and on the move in our world more than ever. But I don't
assume as much as I used to, I don't say as much either.
Now I am a careful charismatic.[11]

* * *

I think I used to confuse faith with my longing for control, particularly of outcomes. Even now, mine is a lame and fumbling
sort of faith.

Like so many aspects of my spirituality, I am still a bit
in-between, figuring out what I reclaim and what I relinquish,
living with a few unanswered questions while relying heavily

on the few things I do know—and almost all of those can be summed up in my complete and utter confidence in Love.

God is for us, who can be against us?

I spent the first half of my last pregnancy wrestling with God. This was my eighth pregnancy but we only had three children. We had been on a roller coaster, going from high to low to high. There was no heartbeat for too long, and then all of a sudden it was there. Then the baby wasn't moving, long after I normally felt the baby move within me. With my history of miscarriage, we were terrified we were losing another baby before birth. I was holding between hope and despair, clenching both faith and unbelief.

I am a woman of prayer. It sounds boldfaced to write it down, but there it is. I write it anyway. Prayer comes easily to my spirit—perhaps because a former pastor once told us that the same part of us that worries is the part that prays. I knew I could worry constantly, so that meant I could pray constantly.

And so I do. I always have. I move through my day with an awareness of my companionship with the Spirit and we talk always, sometimes even with words. I pray, this is what I do. It feels small, so small, in the face of great pain or sorrow or injustice or uncertainty or even joy, but I pray anyway. I carry people and movements, requests and hearts within me like candlelight that I revisit often to hold in my hands and breathe over in prayer.

I don't believe I can control God through prayer or through faith. I don't believe God is waiting for me to "prove" that I have enough faith or know enough Bible verses to argue the points. In fact, I don't believe in praying with an agenda most of the time.

Yet as the days of waiting for this baby to *just move already* went by, I prayed to or wondered at God, grappled with my questions and my doubt, with my beliefs about the nature and character and heart of our God, and with the very real reality of our fallen world. I felt like a frag- mented woman, believing and un- believing all at once.

I don't believe in praying with an agenda most of the time.

One old-school part of me was going all word-of-faith on this baby: praying Scripture, declaring the Word, binding and loosing all sorts of things, declaring life and not death. You name it, I'd claimed it. Another part of me was already grieving and giving up. Another part of me prayed for belief even while acknowledging my own unbelief. One part of me wondered how I even dared to pray and expect God to move for me when I already had three beautiful children and there are far more important things in the world about which I should be pray- ing, how selfish could I be? Another part of me relinquished outcomes, trusting God implicitly no matter the outcome while simultaneously raging against that very thing. Fearlessly, fear- fully, I prayed for life.

And I prayed for faith. I prayed for faith to believe. I prayed because who else was going to keep praying? Who else was going to stand guard over this small one and hang on for dear life, who else but her mother? This is what we do: we stay even when it makes more sense to give up. I prayed because I wasn't going to give up. I wasn't going to be the one to back down from a fight over my child.

I felt like the annoying woman of persistence from one of Jesus' parables, who stood outside the door of a judge pestering the life out of Him until He gave in with bad grace. Jesus called her a woman of great faith.[12] In those long days of waiting, I call her my only hope.

I couldn't muster up my old definitions of faith, I couldn't pretend that everything would be fine, but I could keep relentlessly hope-knocking as my radical act of faith.

> *I couldn't muster up my old definitions of faith, I couldn't pretend that everything would be fine, but I could keep relentlessly hope-knocking as my radical act of faith.*

Then one Saturday morning, I was lying in bed alone (a rarity) when the little fourth baby finally made her presence known: she shifted and moved within my womb with a small whoosh, and my heart exhaled for the first time in weeks. *There you are,* I breathed. *There you are. I've been waiting for you.* She moved like a fish in water, a rolling and a stretching with natural ease that seemed to say, *What? You were worried?*

I stayed in bed, silent, feeling her move within me like faith—a flutter of a presence, growing. There was plenty of time to tell my husband, my mother, my sister, my friends. Right then, it was time to pray, and every word in my mind and mouth, every flutter was *thank you thank you thank you thankyouthankyouthankyou.*

* * *

Yet, if I say God performed a miracle that time, what does that mean for my other babies, the ones I never got to hold except in my folded-up tea towels? I can't forget them.

Yet if I say that it's just a happy coincidence, am I taking away from the miracle and the glory of God's mighty act toward a seemingly small and ordinary woman and her unborn child?

It's both and it's neither; it's holy ground for that very reason, for the uncertainty and the praise, one in each hand. I can only say that fearless prayer did what it always does: it changed me.

If I say that God performed a miracle this time, what does that mean for my other babies?

Still I wonder about faith and the nature of answered prayer. I still hold my understandings loosely. Faith isn't certainty, I know that by now. If I were certain, I wouldn't need faith.

I think faith is both a gift and a choice, sometimes at the same time. I think it's a confidence in the midst of doubt, it's work, and it's rest. Faith is a risk, and it's gorgeous to leap out into the free fall.

Faith becomes more complicated when we allow our hearts to break. When we become present with and for the suffering of the world, when we begin to pay attention to our own stories and the stories of those alongside us—when we do this, our expectations change and our relationship with signs and wonders changes. But our hope only grows deeper roots, our longing for the Kingdom of God stretches out to the sun, and the Spirit's wind and water and fire seem like manna.

Barbara Kingsolver wrote in her book *Animal Dreams*, "The very least you can do in your life is figure out what you hope for. And the most you can do is live inside that hope. Not admire it from a distance but live right in it, under its roof." [13]

That sounds a lot like Hebrews 11—the original definition of faith. [14] So right now, I think faith is figuring out what I hope for—redemption, wholeness, shalom, justice, love, life, one small baby to live and not die, all of it—and then fearlessly living under that roof.

I will always pray as if this one thing is true: God is for us. And it's worthwhile to keep knocking.

That's all I know about faith for sure.

* * *

In today's world of demonic principalities and powers—like racism and patriarchy, war and poverty, systemic injustice and famine, mindless evil and callous hearts—the need for an empowered church seems too urgent to be ignored any longer. I understand why people who grew up the way I did are wary of the talk of the Spirit: it brings up some very real baggage.

But I still want that Spirit language. I want the experience of tongues and signs and wonders and miracles, and I'm greedy enough to want the gift of faith and wisdom too.

I suspect that we expect too little of the Spirit. It's an overcorrection to what we witnessed twenty years ago, but now we are too wary, too suspicious, too skeptical. We've forgotten what it means to be woken up by the Spirit.

Historically, we have called these Holy Spirit movements "awakenings" in our tradition. We look to the great awakenings of the modern church and the ancient church, we pray for the Church to awaken. And I've come to believe that there is no better word than *awakening* for the activity of the Holy Spirit. Perhaps it's no coincidence that much of the African American community uses the phrase "stay woke" to describe the need to pay attention to the world around us, to remain vigilant in times of turmoil and conflict, to question authority, to be suspicious of the empire that rules and the media's spin—particularly in times of change and reckoning. The Holy Spirit awakening is exactly that: *staying woke*. An empowering for a purpose. Awakenings aren't just for our personal benefit but for the benefit of the entire people of God and for the reconciliation and redemption of the world. Wake up. Wake up. Wake up. See the Spirit breathing among the prophets and the poets, the artists and the disturbers. We've been asleep, we've been passive. I'd love to see a big awakening, absolutely, but I'll settle for a few more of us to simply wake up.

To be honest, I don't think the Holy Spirit looks much like barking dogs or roaring lions, gold teeth or hysterical laughter. I've had a front-row seat for the foolishness, and I am over it. I think the Holy Spirit looks like her fruit: love, joy, peace, patience, kindness, goodness, faithfulness, gentleness, and self-control.[15] I think the Holy Spirit was given to the Church for freedom and wholeness, comfort and counsel, so that love would win in and around and through us. The Spirit is present always: she is the very air we breathe; she doesn't only "show up" in big events or moments or movements. I think the Spirit leads us into humility and simplicity rather than spectacular displays of ostentatious wealth or excess. The Spirit is the God of the vine and the branches; apart from that intimate relationship, we bear no fruit. My prayer is that the Holy Spirit would sweep into our lives with holy disruption, upending our assumptions and privileges, our greed and selfishness, our pride and our stupor. To empower our work and our witness. Like Zechariah 4:6 tells us, not by might, not by power, but by my Spirit, says the Lord.

* * *

This is an imperfect sort of story.

Aren't they all?

Just when I think I'm educated beyond the humble old habits, just when I've theologically proven why everything from cheesy Christian music to children's ministry to blogging is useless and sometimes damaging, my wisdom is disrupted. That Christian children's record shouldn't have "worked" as the great pursuit of God toward our family.

But it did.

I've been thinking about an old story in Acts lately. In the heady early days of the Church, Peter and John were once again arrested for preaching Christ and His resurrection. The High Council was furious and wanted to kill them.

But a wise and well-respected Pharisee named Gamaliel stood up and said something incredibly profound: "Men of Israel, take care what you are planning to do to these men! Some time ago there was that fellow Theudas, who pretended to be someone great. About 400 others joined him, but he was killed, and all his followers went their various ways. The whole movement came to nothing. After him, at the time of the census, there was Judas of Galilee. He got people to follow him, but he was killed too, and all his followers were scattered. So my advice is, leave these men alone. Let them go. If they are planning and doing these things merely on their own, it will soon be overthrown. But if it is from God, you will not be able to overthrow them. You may even find yourselves fighting against God!" [16]

I'm a recovering know-it-all. It seems that just when I finally have an opinion locked into place, exceptions abound. Black-and-white thinking has been denied me repeatedly. Some days, I can't figure out if this is a cross to bear or a mercy to enjoy.

The Spirit always sweeps into my opinions and preferences with holy disruption.

Now I've lived through enough evolutions of myself and enough transformation by the Spirit that I have learned to keep my mouth shut a bit more, to wait in kindness, to hold it loosely. I try to think critically without giving myself over to a critical heart. I try to be kind, to remember the ways that I have grown and changed, the ways that I will continue to grow and change and continue to sort it out.

> *I've lived through enough evolutions of myself and enough transformation by the Spirit that I have learned to keep my mouth shut a bit more.*

No matter how hard I try to find a different and more "elevated" path, I always end up circling like a corkscrew back around the same truths I learned at the beginning, my charismatic practices only enriched by the wisdom and practices of ancients through the ages and the prophets alongside of me now, by my study and my sorrow.

Gerard Manley Hopkins wrote that Christ plays in ten thousand places.

> *For Christ plays in ten thousand places,*
> *Lovely in limbs, and lovely in eyes not His*
> *To the Father through the features of men's faces.*[17]

Is it such a stretch to believe He's played so beautifully in my history? Is it such a stretch to believe that the Spirit moved into a family and changed everything because a fourteen-year-old babysitter gave away a children's record from the seventies? What about in a megachurch pastor's sunny sermons? In a television show about prosperity preachers? In our pet theologians and favorite scapegoats and Twitter-sparring contests? In a seminary ivory tower? In Alcoholics Anonymous? In the liturgy? In the old habits of the quiet morning hour spent in Scripture? In tongues and Awanas? In the Baptists and the Presbyterians and the Vineyard and the anti-institutional movement? In the vacation Bible schools and accountability groups? In the stadiums filled with passionate young people singing songs to a jumbo screen with the name of JESUS in artistic sans serif font? In the atheists and agnostics? In the healing lines and the ones praying in tongues? In the powerful and the powerless alike?

I'm learning to move a bit more slowly. Maybe the "next big thing" will come to nothing. Maybe the old thing that once was turned out to be nothing. But maybe, just maybe, Christ is playing there too. And maybe, see, God is doing a new thing, now it springs up, do you not perceive it?[18]

From the mundane to the mountaintop, resurrection hides in the foolish places, it seems.

According to the "experts," these imperfect people or methods or tactics or habits shouldn't work. We've grown out of them, surely. Put such childish things behind us. We are wise, nuanced, well educated now. Right? These ways are sometimes crass, sometimes misguided, sometimes lame. And worse, sometimes they are truly damaging, evil even, and we are left trying to untangle ourselves from the wreckage of someone else's god.

Perhaps we can now admit: we would have done things differently . . . if we knew then what we know now. The old ways of our history are often foolish when we strip them down. And yet they continue to confound the wise.

Christ played in our foolish ways. Christ plays there now. And Christ will continue to play there.

It's an imperfect sort of story. And that makes it all the more beautiful to me.

Obey the Sadness

ON GRIEF AND LAMENT

My friend buried her newborn son. On the night of the memorial service, I drove home alone. I could only hold back that lung-deep cry for so long before I knew it was time to pull over my minivan. To lay my forehead on the steering wheel, keening at the side of the road for a longed-for boy with red hair.

What is there to say? What can we do but huddle into rows of chairs and clutch our hearts and sob into our shredded, balled-up tissues? What can we do but stand around and drink juice, red-eyed and hiccuping? We'll sign up to deliver a few meals when what we really want to do is lay out on the floor beside his mother and cry until we're empty, because what else? There aren't old stories to tell, no laughter breaking through the sorrow. This is lament. Is there really comfort in the idea of a baby in the arms of Jesus when all we want is for that baby to be in the arms of his broken mama?

Psalmists failed to capture this kind of despair. Mothers, fathers, grandparents, friends, weeping for their children, little boys without a brother, babies who are no more. And I want to dig a hole with my bare hands and stay there in a field and in the damp cold, and tell the world that I am so angry, so sad, so longing, I can hardly breathe.

I was wearing black for my friend's baby son. Can anyone face the sight of a soft baby blanket carefully laid out on the altar? *This is not the end, this is not the end*, I was singing the words from Gungor's song "When Death Dies"[1] over and over through the hot tears and the white grief. An illuminated rainbow arched impossibly bright above my head before dropping into the wet green forests, and the rain was still falling through the tired golden light, and the sun was breaking through somewhere behind me, but right then, it was not enough. So I pulled over the minivan, opened the windows, breathed in and out: too much, too much, it's too much, this is too much. *This is not the end.*

* * *

I have an uneasy relationship with death and suffering, with grief and lament. Perhaps it's because, as I told you earlier, my faith tradition is more comfortable with the light of certainty than the darkness of mystery and questions. Our narratives celebrate the simple wins and victories, not the complex heartache. As a people, we prefer stories with a clear beginning, middle, and end. We like our testimonies to end on a high note: and they lived happily ever after. Evil was defeated. Good won. The heroes faced conflict and were victorious. The end.

Turns out life isn't a Disney movie.

* * *

"The weight of these sad times we must obey, and must obey just because they are sad times, sad and bewildering times for people who try to hold on to the Gospel and witness to it somehow when in so many ways the weight of our sadness all but crushes the life out of it," writes Frederick Buechner.[2]

I'm learning to obey the sadness—not only of our times, as Buechner said, riffing on a line from Shakespeare's *King Lear*, but the sadness in my own heart and the sadness of our community and the sadness of our world, and this is hard for me.

Our culture makes little space for the mess. We are expected to have it all together. Don't let them see you sweat, keep your dirty laundry and unsanitized stories to yourself, thank you very much. Be successful, look good, feel good.

I never know if it's a nature or nurture aspect of myself, but I'm very good at compartmentalizing. I can put things into boxes in my mind and simply leave them there. When I worked in fast-paced environments, I never brought my work stress home with me; it simply stayed at work. When things were rough in one relationship, I was still able to engage in the rest of life by simply putting it into the proper box in my mind and leaving it there until it was time to address it. I have been able to bear great

I took pride in my self-possession, counting it as righteousness that no one knew my heart was breaking.

stress and grief while still engaging in my life, still taking care of my children, still getting up and functioning throughout the day. Even when I was in the midst of great darkness or grief, most people never knew. I took pride in my self-possession, counting it as righteousness that no one knew my heart was breaking.

But it was precisely *because* of those too-full boxes that my major spiritual awakenings began. My boxes were too full of questions and doubts, too full of criticisms and bitterness, grief and anger and frustrations. I had crammed too much of my very real self into these inadequate compartments in my mind. The crash was real because the compartmentalizing was real.

Secrets make us sick, I've heard. I made secrets out of my questions and doubts and sadness and grief because I didn't know how to simply sit with them. Even now, I fight against the urge to explain or pretend or ignore away the darkness. It's uncomfortable to lean into the pain, to seek God there in the darkness.

I'm too good at pretending. I'm too good at compartmentalizing. I do not obey my sadness. I default to attempts to control instead of the free fall of surrender.

* * *

This might be the dark side of growing up in the whole faith movement of charismatic tradition. We over-realized the very real truth that "our words matter." Of course they matter: speaking life matters. I still teach my children this lesson and strive to remember the power of my tongue. But as a tribe, we over-realized that truth until we didn't know how to feel our feelings.

Only our most overzealous preached it, but it was an unwritten expectation that ran through a lot of our theology: *Don't give in to the darkness, don't name it, don't give it power, don't acknowledge it, don't confess it, don't be sad, don't be mad, don't be despairing, don't pay attention to the monster crouching in the corner.* We believed that our feelings and circumstances had to obey our carefully curated version of the Word of God: we are more than overcomers; the joy of the Lord is our strength; death has no sting. So don't grieve when death comes calling: *They are now with Jesus.* Don't be sick: *Come down with a healing.* Don't be sad: *The joy of the Lord is your strength.*

And I can't tell you the grief I carry still over the people who were caught in the crossfire consequences of that teaching, believing that their darkness or grief or sadness or despair or sickness was their own fault because they simply lacked faith.

When their stories didn't line up with our narrative, they felt shame and eventually disappeared.

Here's this: when I was sad, when I had real, legitimate reasons for grief or despair or anger or any emotion that was perceived as negative or dark, I had nowhere to go. I didn't know how to feel my feelings. And by my refusing to name or acknowledge them, sometimes the darkness simply grew. As my worldview expanded to include more stories than simply my own, as I woke up to the world outside my own experiences, I saw this even more clearly. Look at the real darkness around us: don't pretend it's not real.

> *When I had real, legitimate reasons for grief or despair or anger or any emotion that was perceived as negative or dark, I had nowhere to go.*

* * *

My mother-in-law is a hospice chaplain. Every day of her work-week, she abides with those who are sick or dying or injured; she sits with their families and friends. Most of us run from sadness and pain, but she went back to school after her children were raised precisely because she felt called to sit in those thin places with the hope of Christ, bearing the ministry of simple presence and comfort. She carries sadness that isn't hers to carry because most of us cannot carry these moments alone, and yet there are so few among us who will make peace with our despair.

* * *

I've been thinking of our Jesus. How He took the bread and tore it with His own hands: *This is my body broken for you.* How He poured out the wine: *This is my blood poured out for you.*

First the death, then the resurrection. We like to skip that first part. We like to think we can have the resurrection without the death.

"Abide with me," the Spirit whispers to us.

* * *

I'm still in the early days of holding space to allow the lament to deepen the joy. I still default to a setting of control instead of a posture of surrender. This is the place of my most unanswered questions, my deepest twilight of belief. I hold it loosely. I offer it hesitantly.

Lament is the place of my most unanswered questions, my deepest twilight of belief.

This isn't merely an intellectual discussion. This is not a puzzle to be pieced together, it's a full-immersion baptism.

Bear with me.

After spending her entire three years of life battling a devastating and rare disease, a small girl died. At her funeral, her grieving mother wore marigolds in her hair.

I have rocked on my hands and knees on the living room floor, laboring to give birth to too-soon babies who would be wrapped in tea towels instead of receiving blankets, taken away from me at the hospital for "testing" that revealed no answers.

My husband's best friend—the one who is like a brother to him—is a widower now. His wife died. Their two blond daughters are about the age of our own tinies. We have borne witness with each other in the joys and sorrows of our lives throughout fifteen years of true friendship. She died slowly.

There is nothing to say. There is only what was happening. This is life sometimes. We mustn't pretend or compartmentalize or ignore or placate. Simply obey the sadness. Speak the truth of what is happening. Not the truth you wish were real. Not the truth that ought to be. Not the platitudes or time-worn clichés to minimize grief.

Of course, it's wrong, we weren't meant for this. This isn't shalom.

But this is what is happening—whether it's right in our own homes or halfway around the world—and so we learn to obey the sadness and live into the Gospel by speaking the truth. Whether it's one soul *And so we learn to obey the sadness and live into the Gospel by speaking the truth.* suffering or a communal grief, whether it's systemic suffering of entire people groups or one lonely man burying his wife.

I prayed for healing. Does that surprise you? It does surprise some people. I prayed for healing right up until the end. I don't regret hope. I will never regret even a conflicted faith.

Here is what I think I know:

God's heart for us is shalom—nothing missing, nothing broken, total and whole peace.

But the world is broken. We are broken. This is because

we have the freedom to choose, the agency of a million billion decisions and choices, it's because powers and principalities are at war among us, it's because we live in a fallen world not yet fully redeemed, and then, there's a bit of ambiguity thrown in too.

* * *

I think that's why I began this book with Jesus. Because really, if we want to know what God is like, Scripture tells us to look to Jesus. Jesus was meant to clarify, to answer the questions, to clean up the dirty window through which we try to behold the holy. Hebrews 1:3 states that Jesus is "the radiance of God's glory and the exact representation of His being."

As I sort through my faith, I've come to believe that almost all of our theology—and therefore our practical lives—has its roots in what we believe about the nature and character of God. It all tracks back.

Jesus asked His disciples, "Who do people say that the Son of Man is?" referring to Himself.

"Well," they replied, "some say John the Baptist, some say Elijah, and others say Jeremiah or one of the other prophets."

Then He asked them, "But who do you say I am?"

Simon Peter answered, "You are the Messiah, the Son of the living God."[3]

* * *

Who do you say He is?

And not the proper Sunday-school answer, not the lists of attributes or the memorized Bible verses—not here, not in this place. When we are sorting through our very core self, this isn't the time for the mask of right answers. This is the time for the honesty. In your heart of hearts, in your raw place of grief and suffering, in your rich center of love and redemption, who do you say God is? There, in that place, who is He to you now?

* * *

We mean well, I know we do. When I have experienced loss or grief or suffering, the well-meaning have tried to comfort me with the idea that it was all God's plan, that all of it would be for a greater good. I've even had some folks tell me recently that clearly my work in ministry these days was why God "took" the babies we lost. Praise God, look at how He is "using" my grief in such a beautiful way, because I dare to write about it and talk about it openly, giving other women permission to do so as well. I know people mean well, but I don't believe that. God can take anything that was meant for evil and turn it for our good—not the least of which is our own character and holiness, our growth and our compassion and our ministry, of course. Sovereignty is redemption, it's not causation.

Whether it's in my own small stories or in the larger and more horrific stories of others, too often we seek to comfort with the plat-

Sovereignty is redemption, it's not causation.

itudes that have held the Church captive for years: God is all-powerful, God could have stopped it, God didn't stop it, therefore this—all this—is God's plan for us. And so this is how we comfort the grieving, the abused, the oppressed, the beaten, the exhausted, the broken.

The problem with this quick shot of comfort, the predigested talking points spouted in times of unspeakable pain, is that they end up filling our heads with the wrong idea of God while perhaps absolving us of our complicity. We pit our pain against

God, holding tally and requiring meaning, instead of saying the truth: *This isn't God's will.* This is completely against what God wants for us. And it's wrong. Wrong. Wrong.

We pit our pain against God, instead of saying the truth: This isn't God's will. The other option is to blame God actively. God sent that hurricane or that earthquake as a punishment for sin. God didn't save your child because the child was unrepentant. God won't answer your prayers because you have unresolved sin in your life or because our society is so incredibly evil. People take Scripture and twist it against our hearts, making us believe that God is to blame for our suffering or that our sin compels His holiness against us.

* * *

I come at this from a bit of a different place than most modern Christians, perhaps because I grew up with a deep knowledge of God's goodness. I was schooled from a young age in the belief that God is good and that all goodness comes from His hands. I was taught that sickness and disease, war and devastating poverty, oppression and evil were the work of the devil, that these things were the very things from which God came to save us.

This was one of the great gifts of my tradition: I'll hang on to this one as worthy in value far beyond my comprehension.

But just as my brothers and sisters in the Church have had to untangle themselves from their notion of God as the possible origin of evil, I've had to untangle myself from the belief that evil or suffering is always the fault of someone's lack of faith. Our strengths often come with a shadow side.

When I really began to depart from the Word of Faith teachings of my childhood, I left behind the promise of guaranteed outcomes. I can't buy that anymore. I have seen too many people go down fighting—people who loved the Lord, who, in anyone's estimation, "deserved" a miracle, people who played by our arbitrary proof-texted rules for answered prayer. We blamed the sufferer because we believed the only other alternative was to blame God.

Who is to say what is more damaging? To hear that God is to blame for your suffering or to hear that you are to blame for it?

Sometimes that might be true: we absolutely may be at fault for our suffering; our suffering may be the consequence of our own sin or choices. But in actuality, much of our suffering is independent from

We blamed the sufferer because we believed the only other alternative was to blame God.

our choices. We suffer at the hands of another, we suffer because of the actions of another, we suffer because this is what it means to be human and live.

Simply blaming God or blaming ourselves fails to recognize the truth that we are in a war zone. The world is complex, ambiguous at times, and so yes, evil things often happen because we live in a fallen world of free agents. We don't always escape the evil in this world, and we don't always find victory in this life, but the core belief I was given at the start is true: God is not to blame.

I didn't learn how to lament and grieve, how to pray and be in community until I learned that God could be trusted. God is against the evil and suffering in the world. He is not the origin of evil nor does He "use" evil as a means to justify some cosmic end. Rather, God fights evil.

I couldn't trust God if I suspected God was behind our deepest griefs and injustices. This is where the sovereignty arguments break down for me. I don't blame God for much any-more. I see God as the rescue from the injustices, not the cause

———————————————— of them. I see God as the redeemer

I see God as the redeemer   of the pain, not the origin of it. I
of the pain, not the origin   see the promise of sovereignty not
of it.   as hypercontrol over the minute

———————————————— and painful details of the world,

but as a faithful promise that all things will be restored, all things will be redeemed, all things will be rescued.

And again, I go back to our Jesus.

When Jesus was confronted with people who suffered, He never offered the platitudes, did He? There was no "everything happens for a reason" or "God has a plan, you just have to wait." There was no "the Lord gives and takes away" or "greater good" of proper theology and doctrine's triumph. Instead, Jesus offered compassion, even tears at times, and here is the amazing thing: Jesus often confronted the suffering of people—whether physical or mental or emotional or spiritual—with healing. God's will was to heal and to make well. We aren't meant to accept these things as God's will: God didn't plan for my babies to die or for our friend to die or for Haiti's earthquake and subsequent cholera outbreak, for horrendous abuse and evil in the world, for any oppression or heartbreak in humanity.

Rather, as the people of God—the ones whose citizenship lies in the Kingdom of God—we are part of the resistance of those things, the overcoming of them, the redemption and hope in the midst of them. Why? Because *that* is God's heart. *That* is God's nature.

In Christ, we learned the truth: "Jesus didn't come to declare that everything already manifests the Father's will. He came, rather, to establish the Father's will, because the world as it now is doesn't consistently manifest God's will," writes Greg Boyd.[4]

The Kingdom of God is being established in this world, absolutely, but it's foolish to think that this is happening through rainbows and unicorns. Instead, Scripture teaches us that we are at war—not against people but against powers and principalities.[5] With our freedom comes risk. We are prophesying the Kingdom of God in our victories and in our defeats. We aren't immune from suffering or excused from the experience of being human simply because of our faith. I only wish that were true.

And the truth remains: the crucified God, as personified in Jesus, revealed that God is always on the side of suffering wherever it is found[6] and God's endgame is resurrection.

* * *

Sovereignty is a promise, not a threat. I no longer think of God's sovereignty as what theologians call a "blueprint" plan for humanity. I can't say things like "Well, God ordained you to be poor." Or "God ordained for your baby to die." I know that some people find comfort in believing that God's sovereignty, His plan for all things, is behind their suffering and grief. It gives meaning to our grief, I get that. But I don't think it's true. In fact, I think that's a crappy thing to say and a crappy thing to believe about God.

God's sovereignty is not an excuse or a reason for the bad things that happen in our lives: God is light, and there is no darkness to Him. No one will ever convince me that God made my babies die or that God killed our friend with cancer or that a hurricane is an act of God as punishment for sin. Instead, I think sovereignty is the promise that it will all be healed in the end. Sovereignty means that all will be held. That God is at work to bring redemption and reconciliation, that somehow at the end of all things, we don't escape from the goodness that pursues us, the life we are promised, the love that redeems.

Sovereignty means that God is at work to bring redemption and reconciliation, that somehow at the end of all things, we don't escape from the goodness that pursues us, the life we are promised, the love that redeems.

* * *

I don't have the answers yet. I don't know that anyone really does. If they claim to have the answers, they're usually selling something. Or so it seems.

We're often given two options: we can blame God or we can blame ourselves. My response to the age-old questions of evil and suffering and grief is no longer arguments and answers and platitudes. Instead, I've turned to a lost practice among us: lament.

I am learning that it is okay to feel sad and to be angry, to long for rescue and redemption, to pray and shout and cry, to weep with those who weep.

Right along with my activism and my faith, right along with my best hopes and my busy hands, my surrender and my prayers, I am learning to simply sit in the sadness and allow it to be there with me. I am learning not to pretend that sadness doesn't exist or that it has an easy answer or that God is to blame. I'm learning to not avoid it or ignore it.

I am learning to lament, to mourn, to weep with those who weep, to take our shared sadness and bewilderment into my own soul too.

It's okay to feel it.

It's okay and it's necessary, it's holy and good work. We need to listen to the stories that make us uncomfortable and challenge our peace. As Christians, I think it's our responsibility to carry each other's burdens and be a part of restoring justice

———————————

It's okay to feel it.

———————————

for one another. Sometimes that means being able to carry truly terrible truths without letting them bury us whole.

Sometimes the most holy work we can do is listen to each other's stories and take their suffering into our hearts, carrying each other's burdens and wounds to Christ together, in faith and in lament, together.

I've learned that faith isn't pretending the mountain isn't there. It isn't denial of the truth or the facts or the grief or the anger. It's not the lie of speaking "peace, peace" when there is no peace.[7] It's faith because it is hope declared, it is living into those things that are not yet as they will be.

I hold space for the righteous anger and the grief. I join in the lamentations of the weary world.

And then I will seek ways to embody those very prayers, to incarnate them, to further heaven's hopes and summon God's glory in ways big and small, seen and unseen, mundane and holy.

* * *

The night that our friend's wife died, my brokenhearted husband called his mother: *What do I say? What do I do? What will fix this? There is nothing else to do. You do this every day, Mom: what do I do for my friend?*

Now is the time to sit with Him, she said.

There is nothing to say. Stop thinking there is something to

say to make it go away. It won't go away. Abandon your answers.
Avoid your clichés. Don't blame God and don't blame him.

Abandon your answers. Avoid your clichés. Don't blame God and don't blame him. Learn to sit in the sadness.

Learn to sit in the sadness. *This is not the end, this is not the end.*

He booked a ticket to Colo-rado, and he flew to his friend.
He stayed with him, day after day after day, doing the things with him that needed to be done. At
night, together, they put the motherless girls to bed, and then
they sat outside, usually in silence, looking up at the sky, still
alive.

Beautiful Facade

ON JUSTICE AND SHALOM

On my most recent trip to Haiti, I saw a beautiful hillside of
colorful houses. We pulled our van over and took pictures of
the cheery homes: purple, orange, apple green, sky blue. It
made me happy to see the colorful homes among the usual
cacophony of gray cinder block in post-earthquake Haiti. I
thought it might be a public art project. But I also wondered
why not all the houses on the hillside were painted. There was
a line, almost straight down the hill, dividing the tiny houses
that were painted bright colors from the usual slums. But
the painted houses were so pretty, and so I took pictures and
posted them on Instagram. "I want to frame that and put it on
my wall," I said.

Then our translators and local friends told us the truth: it
was Jalousie. A shanty town for the poor and destitute disguised
with paint. There was no running water, no sewage system, no
electricity except what is illegally tapped in. The government
painted one exterior wall of these homes bright colors. Critics
say that the homes of Jalousie were painted because their slum
faces the rich part of town, the place where people like me

come and stay in lovely hotels—a PR campaign to the tune of 1.4 million dollars.[1]

After all, everybody knows the rich white folks don't want to look at ugly gray cinder block shanties. It ruins supper on the terrace.

That entire story is pretty much a metaphor for my experiences in justice work. I'm well-meaning but ignorant. I only know the stories I'm told, and too often I long for a quick-fix happy ending. When I heard the truth of the painted houses of Jalousie, my stomach sank. Because I'd fallen for the beautiful facade. Again.

These moments remind me to keep my mouth shut, to listen, to dig a bit deeper, beyond the facades, to look past the shiny bright exterior and into the home, into the streets, into the truth.

It's easy to fall for the bright colors because we want so badly to believe in a good and resolved story. We want the good guys to win—quickly.

But spend any amount of time working toward justice and you learn to become distrustful of the shiny, pretty, easy answers. You become a bit suspicious of the facades. You learn to peek behind the story and poke it with a stick. You learn to ask real questions of the real people, not the PR team. You grow tired of short-term quick-fix thinking in lieu of investing in the long game with preventative measures of community and economic development.

It's hard to settle for more dingy, half-peeling-off Band-Aids when you're longing for a full healing.

It's hard to settle for more dingy, half-peeling-off Band-Aids when you're longing for a full healing.

There isn't much room for romanticism in the real world of justice and peacemaking.

* * *

For someone who grew up memorizing and reading the Bible, I was quite ignorant of God's heart for justice. Whenever I get sniffy about how much I know the Bible, I remember how long it took me to realize that God made this whole do-justly-love-mercy thing pretty clear to us throughout the Bible, and yet I missed it for so long.

Perhaps that's the problem with cherry-picking Bible verses for our personal lives: we miss the bigger and more beautiful story of what God is doing in the world. We make the story about ourselves instead of seeing ourselves as part of the big story.

It wasn't until I relearned how to read my Bible and learned about the Kingdom of God that I began to see God's love for the oppressed, the hopeless, the margin-alized, the forgotten, the least powerful, the widow, the poor, the immigrant.

> *We make the story about ourselves instead of seeing ourselves as part of the big story.*

Ken Wytsma defined *justice* as the "single best word, both inside and outside the Bible, for capturing God's purposes for the world and humanity's calling in the world. Justice is, in fact, the broadest, most consistent word the Bible uses to speak about what ought to be, and it has been used throughout the centuries by Christians and non-Christians alike to describe vital areas of human and divine concern."[2]

I'm a social justice wannabe. My heart has awakened to

God's heart for justice, but I'm still figuring out what that means in my life and what my life might mean in the world. I am learning, painfully, just how complicated and nuanced these conversations can be.

Justice is a bit of a buzzword in the Church these days. We can sometimes fool ourselves into thinking that we're actually doing justice simply because we're *talking* about justice. We like to talk a lot about justice because the actual doing of it is terrifying. And tiring. And ordinary. And inconvenient. And countercultural.

Justice is often born in the quiet and ordinary moments long before it's seen by anyone else. Sometimes it's as simple and as difficult as listening, as learning, as laying down our excuses or justifications or disguises, as forgiveness, as choosing the hard daily work of restoration, as staying resolutely alive when everyone else is numbing themselves against it.

Keep caring. Let yourself be angry. Let your heart be broken. Let yourself be uncomfortable.

Keep caring. Let yourself be angry. Let your heart be broken. Let yourself be uncomfortable.

Eugene Cho writes that "God invites and commands His people to not just be aware of injustice but to pursue justice. Not just to pursue justice but to live justly. These two acts are not the same, but they are inseparable. To be followers of Jesus, we are required to pursue justice and live justly at the same time."[3]

It was precisely because I reoriented my life around Jesus and following Him, apprenticing myself to His way of life, that I woke up to God's heart for justice and redemption After all, God's heart for justice doesn't start and end with me or you: it includes the entire world, and we're missing it mightily if we reduce the Gospel to a personal salvation experience.

The funny thing about justice, about having your heart awaken to God's heart for humanity, is that you set out to change the world and run smack into the truth that you yourself need to be saved too.

You set out to change the world and run smack into the truth that you yourself need to be saved too.

* * *

When I start getting mad at the facade, I peek behind it and guess who I find?

The Church.

The people of God are already there, among the poor, serving the poor, loving the ones behind the beautiful colorful lies. They've just been waiting for the rest of us. I think there's a way to be a critical thinker without having a critical spirit. I think there's a way to help without hurting.

The comfort of the divine is this: *Do not be afraid.* Over the years, God has gracefully, wholly, generously, ferociously, broken the chains of fear in my life. And now I know that fear must always be cast out and that the only fix, the only key, is love. Love is greater than fear; love always wins.

Now I know that fear must always be cast out and that the only fix, the only key, is love.

I want to love the poor, and I also need to recognize my own poverty, my own complicity in systems of injustice. I don't want to make caricatures or sob stories or manipulations or success stories out of another person. I would like to love. I would like to meet my neighbors both next door and in the developing world, to know them. Justice isn't for "over there": it's for here and now and all of us. And I'd like to learn, and I'd like to help, if I can, and I don't know where else to start but right where I am, right now. The Spirit often calls us to repentance before we are called to our ideas of revolution.

* * *

I can be a bit cynical about people out to change the world now. For instance, when I was first invited to go to Haiti with an organization called Help One Now to be a "storyteller" years ago, I wanted to say no. Of course, there were practical reasons: it's far away, inconvenient, and my children were very young. But I also wanted to say no because I have an aversion to the whole blogger/celebrity trip phenomenon in nonprofit circles. So when Chris, the leader of the Help One Now tribe, asked me to join him on a short trip to Haiti with a few other bloggers to "tell stories," my first instinct was a simple no.

The western world, including churches, has a habit of showing up in developing countries with a lot of zeal and good intentions that can ultimately end up hurting or crippling complex societies, and then wounding precious people through inadvertent ignorance. I have learned by now that helping can hurt,[4] and I didn't want to hurt Haiti economically or relationally. I wasn't interested in tidy, simple narratives for the purpose of raising money. I cringed at the thought of trotting Haitians out as props for fund raising. The phrase "poverty tourism" revolted me. It was easier and safer to do, well, *nothing*.

God is already at work in every corner of the world, in new and beautiful ways, and we have much to learn *from* Haiti. God did not arrive in Haiti with the mission trippers and NGOs.

I believe that *how* we do a thing is as much a part of justice as the result of it all.

Yet I couldn't seem to say no to going to Haiti.

Every time I tried to refuse, my *no* stuck in my throat. I wondered if that might be a nudge from the Holy Spirit, so I took a few steps back, and as I got to know Chris and the rest of the team, I learned they were centered on empowering and resourcing local leaders for the long haul, precisely because of their great love for God. They were focused on community development to combat the orphan crisis, instead of simple rescue aid or hugging orphans one week and then disappearing once the slide-show pictures were done. Their intent was not to have feel-good "revivals" to fluff up statistics in church annual reports. Chris and his team deferred to Haitian leaders and purposefully kept all non-Haitians associated with the project in the background. They took the posture of students, listeners, fellow journeyers—not saviors. They didn't shy away from the complexities of Haiti's systemic injustices and the long road ahead. They were not perfect, but they were learning, because they were there to stay with Haiti.

So I said yes.

I went to Haiti. I've heard that souls grow by leaps and bounds. If that is true, then Haiti was a catapult for me. Chris and his team were not show-up-and-take-pictures Christians; they were we-are-with-you-always-especially-in-the-hard-parts Christians. They thought about the long-term consequences of their decisions; they thought about community development that was driven by relationships.

The Kingdom of God is a seed, a grain of wheat; the Kingdom of God is a treasure in a field, it's leaven in the bread, it's a feast and a wedding and a party, it's the forever way. There is no flash-in-the-pan performance with God's ways. And the people of God are salt and light, a city on a hill. Kingdom of God people stay when everyone else leaves to the next sexy project or cause.

The people of God love, they push back the darkness together, they freely give honor and dignity. They make friends.

The people of God's Kingdom come back. They learn before they teach, they listen, and they stay.

I'm learning to stay. I'm learning to listen.

* * *

The first time I went to Haiti, I met a man who moved a mountain. Literally.

After the earthquake hit Haiti, much of the already-shaky infrastructure was damaged or destroyed, particularly around the capital city, Port-au-Prince. One of the local leaders turned his home into an orphanage overnight: abandoned or orphaned children kept showing up at his house, and as he said, "What was there to do but let them in?" After the years had gone by, he began to realize that many of the children in their community were vulnerable to child traffickers or the *restavek* system in Haiti.[5] Pastor Gaetan began to consider the simple solution of creating a school. In addition to educating children out of poverty and ignorance, he felt that this would be a safe place for children while their parents worked during the day. He had enough space at his home to build a school in the yard, but the land was unusable. A steep hill of rock and solid Haitian yellow clay made building impossible. The hill was expensive to excavate owing to a lack of workers and equipment. As the word passed that Gaetan wanted to build a school but couldn't because of the steep hill in the backyard, one sixty-year-old man showed up.

One man with a pickax and a shovel and a bucket. With only lunch for payment, he began to dismantle that mountain, stone by stone. In the blazing heat without benefit of shade, he single-handedly dismantled that entire mountain and smoothed the ground for a school to be built.

We told his story on our blogs, and then we raised the money to build the school. It's been a few years since he gave his strength and energy, time and sweat to that rock demolition.

And today, there are approximately 250 children at that school. I returned a couple of years later, and I stood in the exact spot where that hillside had stood—except now I was standing in a classroom.

I now feel like I've been witness to the miracle, the miracle of the Church united across nations, the Church that shows up and loves well, the Church that stretched from

I stood in the exact spot where that hillside had stood—except now I was standing in a classroom.

my little home in Abbotsford all the way to Haiti—and then to homes across the world in Ireland, Australia, the United States, and beyond.

The school was not simply aid, nor was it a handout or an invasion. No, this was a Haitian-led community development plan born out of friendship and relationship.

This school is one small thing, one small stone in that massive mountain of complex issues related to economics, social justice, community development, family, debt repayments, international policy, poverty, education, all of it.

I couldn't move the whole mountain. But I could help move

one stone, and I chose this small stone because Chris and his team of people who live there told me it was a good pick.

Sometimes, yes, we do speak to a mountain and it will lift up and be cast into the sea. But I've also learned over my lifetime that it is just as holy and just as ridiculous and just as miraculous for the people of God to pick up their own small shovels and get to work, a million small stones at a time.

I have decided that, rather than being someone who denies the existence of the mountain entirely—whatever that represents in the moment—or someone who simply gives up in despair, I will be a woman who picks up small stones and moves them. Small acts of faith and justice are still acts of faith and justice. I will be a woman who slowly and over time and alongside many others will make that mountain move.

Small acts of faith and justice are still acts of faith and justice.

Revolution doesn't look like changing diapers or making meals, right? Kind people don't change the world. We can't imagine overturning the empire through these small stones that we lift up, one after another, through the small lives we minister to, through our words and our prayers.

But some of the most Christlike people I have known in my life, the ones who have changed the world, are doing it in ways that we often think are beneath us. I know we're dazzled by social media platforms and conference stages, bullhorns and accolades, faraway locations and long plane rides. We take liberties with them, perhaps.

Jesus often spoke of the Kingdom of God in small ways: a seed that grows to a mighty oak, a bit of yeast that causes the whole loaf to rise. I have a preference for the grassroots folks, I admit. I see the ones far from the usual power and leadership narratives as the heroes.

And so I believe that we—as the people of God—are called to prophetically live out the Kingdom of God in our right-now lives. That means setting up our lives as an outpost for the Kingdom way of life, the life of a disciple, the life and life-more-abundant of our God's dream for humanity.

The Kingdom is often taking root in small ways—in our kitchens and in our parish halls, in our streets and our sub-sidized daycares, in youth group mentoring relationships and after-school care, in prayer circles and bylaw meetings at city council.

* * *

Whether it's racism, patriarchy, warmongering, greed, or child trafficking, it's counter to God's Kingdom. But the people caught in those systems are rarely the enemies; often they are just as caught, as longing for a rescue as the rest of us. We don't battle against flesh and blood, not really, but against the powers and principalities that hold us all captive.

My friend Kelley tells me that sometimes we think we're called to fighting but really we're called to farming. And if we're called to farming, this very nonsensical expression of discipleship might bump up against our need for power. It's all very well to talk about "the upside-down Kingdom of God" until that discipleship asks us to actually live it out in behind-the-scenes ways.

To the world, it's foolish to choose peace instead of war. It's foolish to forgive. It's foolish to be kind. It's foolish to hope. It's foolish to offer grace and conversation. It's foolish to care for our weaker brothers or sisters, let alone change our own behavior to accommodate their growth and discipleship, their freedom and their journeys. It's foolish to live without legalism and "clear boundaries." It's foolish to make it our business to pursue a quiet life. It's foolish to lay down our power. It's foolish to be silent and listen to others instead of rushing to make our own point. It's foolish to recognize our own privilege and walk softly. It's foolish to honor one another.

Foolish things will confound the "wise" of our world.

Those things all do seem foolish to me. So much of what Jesus and the early church calls me to in Scripture seems foolish to the world. They confound me. They often go against my very real instincts to burn down bridges and shut down dissent and pick fights and turn over tables and draw lines in the sand. But I think that when we are foolish in the ways of a disciple, we live prophetically in the Kingdom of God.

We can prophesy a better world with our very words and actions.

The Spirit transforms our hearts and minds and then our lives—regardless of our past, regardless of our context, regardless of our privilege or lack thereof. If we are disciples, we are participating in the life of Jesus now. And the way in which we engage in our lives matters. The way in which we engage our enemies matters even more, perhaps.

This is how we will be known: by our love.

I want my work and witness to be marked by whom I build up, not whom I tear down. I want to be known as one who speaks life, not death, one who empowers and affirms and speaks even the hard truth in love and invitation. I want us to be the ones who boldly deconstruct and then, with grace and intention and inclusion, reconstruct upon the Cornerstone. I want to embody the character and nature of the Kingdom of God, of our holy God, even when it seems so foolish.

I guess I'm foolish enough to believe that they will know us by our love.

I don't want to be swallowed by the darkness. Nor do I want to be blinded by the beautiful facade. No, I want to be part of a people who see the darkness, know it's real, and then, then, then, *light a candle anyway.* And hold that candle up against the wind and pass along our light wherever it's needed from our own homes to the halls of legislation to the church pulpit to the kitchens of the world.

Finally, I think one of the most important things I can hang on to as I follow Jesus through this world is hope. In fact, I've come to see hope as a radical act of faith and courage, an embodiment of the Kingdom, and vital to our work for justice.

I believe in the redemptive movement of God, moving the story of humanity further into God's purposes and heart for us, one story at a time. I have faith in the soon-coming Kingdom and I believe we know how the story ends—all things restored, all tears wiped from our eyes, love wins—and because of the millions of places where heaven is already breaking through on earth.

I have hope because I believe in the power of the grass roots, because I believe in the little ones and the little ways. I have hope because of the unnamed and unnoticed and uncelebrated disciples in our world who simply get on with it. We are engaged in the reality of living out the hope of glory in our real, right-now lives in the trenches. We are serving our communities, teaching kids to read, taking meals to the elderly and sick, inviting immigrants to share the Christmas table. We are

206 Out <i>of</i> Sorts

leading Bible studies in prisons and praying for the sick and rescuing girls from brothels in Thailand and telling the truth behind the beautiful facade and passing Kleenex across the kitchen table when our friend's marriage falls apart.

I'm not always hopeful. Sometimes I'm discouraged and angry, wanting once again to just peace out and leave the crazies behind. But I can't quite walk away. I can't bring myself to abandon hope.

In the pursuit and work of justice, hope is subversive.

Hope isn't withdrawal or blind ignorance; it's not burying our heads in the sand and singing about Gospel ships coming to take us away, nor is it pretending that *it's fine, we're fine, everything's fine.*

Many things in our world are not fine. Hope dares to admit that.

Theologian and scholar Walter Brueggemann writes beautifully in *The Prophetic Imagination* that real hope comes only after despair. Only if we have tasted despair, only if we have known the deep sadness of unfulfilled dreams and promises, only if we can dare to look reality in the face and name it for what it is, can we dare to begin to imagine a better way.

Hope is subversive precisely because it dares to admit that all is not as it should be.

And so we are holding out for, working for, creating, prophesying, and living into something better—for the Kingdom to come, for oaks of righteousness to tower, for leaves to blossom for the healing of the nations, for swords to be beaten into plowshares, for joy to come in the morning, and for redemption and justice.

12

Evangelical Hero Complex

ON VOCATION AND CALLING

Before I was a stay-at-home mum and a writer, I was in financial services marketing for a major American bank. Very early in our marriage, I was offered an opportunity for a cross-country move from where we lived near San Antonio to Boston or New York. As a western Canadian kid who had devoured novels about New York writers, and as a lifelong Boston Bruins hockey fan, I was dazzled at the idea of living and working in either city. I figured even if we just went for five or ten years, it would be the experience of a lifetime. I wanted to say yes.

But when I went home to tell my very young new husband about the opportunity, his immediate reaction was to say "No way." It wasn't because he didn't want to live in those places: he did. It wasn't because he had any weirdness about me being the primary breadwinner in our home: that had already been happening for a while. It wasn't because he was scared: he was always more adventurous than me when it came to following what we then perceived as the will of God. It wasn't because we structured our marriage in such a way that he was the head and I was the submissive wife: right from the early days, our marriage was egalitarian in nature and practice.

He wanted me to turn down the opportunity because he was in full-time vocational ministry and I was not. Being a youth pastor was far more important than working at a bank, you see, because he was doing "the work of the Lord" while I had a regular job. I was a layperson, he was a minister. Ministry life trumped "regular life" every time.

Ministry life trumped "regular life" every time.

Of course, he was right. How could I have even considered this move? Of course his role as a youth pastor was more important than anything else. Of course we would build our entire lives around his call as a pastor.

"If you are called to be a pastor, don't stoop to be a king," my husband used to say to the young students in his care. He was repeating the exact phrases he had been told when he was a teenager. Right from the time he himself was the age of these kids, he had never considered a "regular job"; he was only ever and always going to be "in ministry." Anything else would be settling for less. All his authority figures and influencers affirmed this decision.

I said no to that East Coast opportunity and stayed put in the San Antonio office. I don't have any regrets about it now, because life has unfolded in a good way for us. But now, when we look back on that moment in our marriage, we both feel a profound sense of disbelief: *Who were those people?*

Sometimes we laugh when we talk about our old "evangelical hero complex"—possibly the kind of laughing that you do to keep from crying. We truly believed that the best and truest and most holy way to serve God was through full-time vocational ministry. From the time we were teenagers, we were both overchurched and overprogrammed and burning out. Like many young products of the evangelical church and particularly our little branch of charismatics, we had divided our lives into sacred and secular compartments. We defined ministry exclusively as "sacred work" and it was specific to things like preaching or leading programs at church. We believed in working hard for the Church. We learned to preach, to lead Bible studies, to lead short-term mission trips, to fit our gifts or talents or skills into a narrow understanding of ministry.

We truly believed that the best and truest and most holy way to serve God was through full-time vocational ministry.

The ones who were really serious about God were in full-time vocational ministry. Everyone else got a regular job because we—meaning me—weren't called in the same way; our role was to finance the Real Work of the Ministry.

Much as someone with a hero complex seeks out opportunities to be a hero, my husband and I sought out opportunities to be evangelical heroes. Do big things for God! Do radical things! Do hard things! You'll reach thousands for Christ! And if you don't, what is your life even worth to God?

And every time I heard that message preached, it subtly communicated something rather wrong to my young heart: if it's not big and audacious and obvious, it's not good enough for God.

Who had time for small faithfulness when there is a big, big God with big, big plans for this generation?

It's no wonder we developed an evangelical hero complex: we were surrounded by hero worship, Christian celebrity, video venues, names in lights, book deals, and big-name preachers. Like any student of mass media communication, I know my

Marshall McLuhan: the medium is the message. And in this case, the medium or habits or central figures of our church experiences communicated a louder message than we could bear. The bigger and more influential and powerful the ministry, the better for the Kingdom of God. Obviously. God liked big and powerful, right? The more influence and resources we had, the more good we could do. Bigger is better. Powerful is better. More resources always equal more good.

* * *

Methodist theologian Thomas Oden writes that "there remains a line as thin as hair, but as hard as a diamond, between ordained ministry and the faithful layperson."[1] And there it is, the distinction on which we cut our teeth: there is a difference between clergy and laity, the two-tier division between those who "do" ministry and those who "receive" ministry.

And who, particularly among the young and impressionable and energetic, wouldn't want to be in the tier that *does* the ministry?

* * *

Early in his adolescence, my husband was called to ministry. For more than twenty-five years, every decision in his life was made around supporting that call. It's an odd word, isn't it? *Called.* We say it so easily because this is the world in which we grew up. We lived in a context that invited and expected the active and intimate involvement of the Holy Spirit in our daily decisions. So when I say that we "felt called," I mean that we believed God wanted us to do that work. This calling was usually affirmed not only in our own hearts and minds and inclinations but through the voices of authority and influence in our lives.

Even as a kid, Brian was a gifted teacher and a charismatic leader; he was outgoing and bright. For fun, he played football and basketball, naturally rising to become captain of both teams at his small school. I tease him still that his high school years were like a real-life Archie comic, complete with his coronation as homecoming king. But underneath that smart jock exterior, with a clear path to successful ministry before him, were the seeds of what lay ahead. He already had a yearning for justice and a lot of questions that defied the scripted answers. He also loved to build things and create through landscaping or carpentry, spending his Saturdays on what he called "projects." His grandpa was a sheet metal worker, a blue-collar man who taught Brian everything he knew.

Me, I've always wanted to be a writer. For years, my career was just how I made a living. Perhaps that's the real reason I was content to let the chance in New York and Boston go— it wasn't my great passion, it was just a good opportunity. I went to work to pay our mortgage, but in the evenings and on the weekends? I wrote. I wrote a blog that nobody read. I scribbled in old journals. I've written compulsively throughout my entire life. It is the one constant for me. I never grew out of writing. I never become bored with it.

Writing was my vocation long before it was a way of paying the bills. And truthfully, even now, I don't pay many bills this way. But I never stop. I could never stop. I will be writing for all my life, and I know this. I wrote long before anyone showed up to read my work, and I will be writing long after the lights go out and everyone goes home. It is my great passion. It is the work that I would do for free. (I know this because I have spent most of my career as a writer doing it for free.) I do it simply because I must and because I love it. This is my own call, I see that now.

Even when he was pastoring full-time, my husband would rather build than do just about anything else. Some men relax by playing video games; he lays hardwood. He has learned everything from finish carpentry to plumbing to electrical work to furniture building. His drywall seams are invisible. His 45-degree corners on baseboards make grown men weep with their beauty. He figures out the right way to do a thing and then he does it. He's renovated our washrooms, laid tile and hardwood floors, rebuilt walls, created doorways. Our house is almost always in the throes of one of his "projects."

* * *

One day while he was refinishing a dresser in our garage, I said to him, "You know, it seems like doing this kind of stuff is for you what writing is for me. You do it for free, just for the love of it." I went on to comment on how he learned everything he could about building and creating, how he did it well—not because someone was grading him or evaluating him, but because he loved to see work done well.

"You should have been a carpenter. I think you missed the boat with the whole pastoring thing," I teased. But as most spouses know, sometimes a casual comment takes root in our minds and refuses to let go.

Later that night, he wondered aloud why nobody in his church or his Christian school or community ever said something like that to him. After all, he's always been like this—always loved having a project, always loved using his hands and his mind together, loved to create, to bring order out of chaos, bring function and beauty to the world.

"Why did no one ever once even suggest to me that I could be a carpenter or a home builder to the glory of God?" he mused.

Answer: They didn't know you could be.

We all thought that the height of success was full-time vocational ministry. There was no room in the narrative for a smart, driven, charismatic young man with a clear heart for God to even consider something other than ministry.

Of course you'll be in ministry. Of course.

* * *

Philosopher Arthur Holmes writes, "If the sacred-secular distinction fades and we grant that all truth is ultimately God's truth, then intellectual work can be God's work as much as preaching the gospel, feeding the hungry, or healing the sick. It too is a sacred task."[2]

Cue the record scratch.

Wait, what? That means all work has the potential to be God's work? Not just preaching? Not just leading in a church context? Not just influential and powerful positions of leadership? Not just a stadium of lights and music and fiery preaching? Could God, in fact, be just as much at work in every vocation? Did God see all of us as equally necessary and important?

* * *

The odd thing is that the idea of clergy versus laity, or ones who minister versus the ones who receive ministry, isn't even found in the teachings of the early church. In fact, the New Testament writers flat-out rejected the common terms *laikos* (which means "belonging to the common people") and *idiotes* (yes, that's the root word for our English word *idiot*) as disparaging and as making false distinctions among the people of God. To them there was no such thing as a common Christian.[3] Jesus Himself said, "But you are not to be called 'Rabbi,' for you have one Teacher, and you are all brothers (Matthew 23:8 NIV).

The big difference is seen between how the Old Testament viewed leadership and how the early church viewed leadership. In Israel, leaders were set apart by anointing, by rules, and by expectations. But in the early church, this system of leadership was dissolved by the Lordship and Headship of Christ. "As God intended to be Himself king over Israel, so Christ has come as God's king over His newly constituted people. As head of His church, all others, including leaders, function as parts of one body both sustained by Christ and growing up into Him."[4]

This was a profound and jarring change for the early church. There isn't a two-tier construction where clergy serve the people or even serve on behalf of the people. Rather, we're called to view the Church as one, as the whole people of God, all of us called and gifted together as a unified whole on mission, each with a vital role.

Paul wrote in 1 Corinthians 12:13, "Some of us are Jews, some are Gentiles, some are slaves, and some are free. But we have all been baptized into Christ's body by one Spirit, and we have all received the same Spirit."[5]

R. Paul Stevens wrote an excellent book called *The Other Six Days: Vocation, Work, and Ministry in Biblical Perspective* that thoroughly rocked our worlds. In it he declares, "The New Testament opens up a world of universal giftedness, universal empowerment of the people of God through the gift of the Holy

Spirit, universal ministry, and the universal experience of the call of God by all the people of God."[6]

Leadership within the Church is often still necessary and important, but this shift in thinking helps us to see that the work of leadership is from among and within, rather than from above or outside, let alone better or more important. All our work has the potential to be the ministry of Christ. In this way, church leadership follows Jesus' model of servanthood, not of "lordship."[7]

Gordon Fee recognizes, "In the New Testament documents leaders are always seen as part of the whole people of God, never as a group unto themselves. . . . Thus the model that emerges in the New Testament is not that of clergy and laity, but of the whole people of God, among whom leaders function in service of the rest."[8] That phrase "service of the rest" doesn't mean that only laity receive ministry as an end in itself *We are equipped by our leaders to do the work of the ministry.* but rather that we are equipped by our leaders to *do* the work of the ministry as described in Ephesians 4:11–12: "He handed out gifts of apostle, prophet, evangelist, and pastor-teacher to train Christ's followers in skilled servant work, working within Christ's body, the church, until we're all moving rhythmically and easily with each other, efficient and graceful in response to God's Son, fully mature adults, fully developed within and without, fully alive like Christ."

* * *

When we first left full-time vocational ministry, we felt like failures. I think it's because so much of our identity was tied up in my husband's job title. Even my own identity was tied up there. I was a pastor's wife, which somehow felt suffocating, defining, and prestigious, all at the same time. I liked the authority it granted to me, the recognition, even the insider status. In my husband's case, not only was "pastor" his identity, it was part of his name. For years, everyone called him Pastor Brian, like it was his first name.

After years preparing to be Pastor Brian and then living as Pastor Brian, it's a bit jarring to suddenly become plain old Brian. Who are you if you don't have your name anymore? Much of our evangelical hero complex was rooted in how we saw ourselves—in our identity.

For us, leaving full-time vocational ministry was basically an identity crisis.

* * *

Over the years, we have had to learn the hard way that everything we do can be for the glory of God. Our work, our play, our advocacy, our lives both inside and outside Sunday morning church. Truth is truth, and it will set you free. Everything we do can be infused with the Spirit.

That realization changed my life.

Suddenly my life wasn't about "ministry life" versus "the rest of my life" or about the never-ending war between them. *Sacred* wasn't as easy to separate from *secular.* I didn't see any separation of my spirituality between going to work and going to church: both were opportunities to move with the Spirit, to embody something prophetic and holy, to bring hope and goodness to one another.

> *Suddenly my life wasn't about "ministry life" versus "the rest of my life."*

This new understanding became especially important to me

when I became a mother. My life slowed down, and it was one of the best things to ever happen to me. I couldn't be the type of mother I wanted to be and run myself ragged for church-approved activities, earning all my stars for God's imaginary star-chart in the sky. When my productivity was removed from spirituality, I learned how beloved we are—apart from what we can do or accomplish for God. In fact, I began to realize that a lot of what I was trying to accomplish for God was actually just me trying to gain recognition and satiate that weird desire to be God's hero.

When my productivity was removed from spirituality, I learned how beloved we are—apart from what we can do or accomplish for God.

I believe in the undivided life. There aren't spiritual things and sacred things, not really. All things can be spiritual, and our most "spiritual" acts can become secular if they aren't infused with the Holy Spirit. We can reduce Christ to a compartment in our lives instead of Lord over it all—our day-to-day decisions, our politics, our theology, our community. Stepping back from earning our salvation through ministry or productivity or platforms or titles meant that we learned how to invite God into our whole lives.

When we invite God's presence into our entire lives as they stand right now, the presence of God becomes like a flame within us, pushing back the darkness, wherever we find ourselves. I am ashamed at how I limited God to my "great sacred acts," to our church services, to worship, to preaching, to Bible study. Instead, when I went for a walk in the wilderness, I found the Spirit alive and active and moving in all corners of humanity. In art, science, literature, nature, marriage, laughter, beauty, work, housekeeping, cooking. I found God in suffering and in grief. I found the people of God out here in the world, quietly getting on with the work of the Gospel, far away from stages and book deals and clear job descriptions and designated parking spots at the front of the church. The Holy Spirit doesn't require titles or 501-3(c) official nonprofit status.

If we see ourselves as N. T. Wright's parables of hope, then wherever we find ourselves tells a story of God.

If we assume we hold the market on God's truth and redemption, we miss all the different ways that God is at work in the world right now. If we narrow the holy vocations to a select few, we turn a blind eye to the places where God is already active in the world. The redemptive movement of God includes all creation. God doesn't need our stamp of approval to be at work. In fact, I have often found evidence of God's presence in the strangest of places, far from our neat and tidy categories. It has reminded me of His vastness, His boundary-shattering love, His wild and terrible habit of including the ones whom I forget. We forget that the line between secular and sacred is man-made. The presence of God can enflame it all.

* * *

I don't think that God really wants to "use" me anymore. I kind of hate that terminology now. I know we mean well, of course we do. We say things like, "Oh, I just want to be used by God!" When we say "used by God," we mean that we want our lives to count for something bigger than ourselves. But the language we use matters. Our words reveal what we truly think and believe about God, don't they? Perhaps it's semantics, molehill-to-mountain making (it wouldn't be the first time I did that, as we all know), but the word *use* when it comes to vocation and calling makes the hackles on the back of my neck bristle, my blood get a bit hot. Here I go: I don't believe God wants to use me. Not in the least.

I wasn't created to be used. We were not saved, set free, rescued, and redeemed to be used. We aren't here to work and earn our way; we aren't pew fodder or a cog. We aren't here to prove how worthy we are for the saving. There isn't anything left to earn. God won't use us up. He doesn't devour all our talents, our gifts, our mind, our love, or our energy but redeems them and brings us joy in the practice of them. Despite our tendency to view ministry as a profession and the work of the Gospel as more precious than our marriages and attendance at school concerts, the truth is that our value to God is not determined by our workhorse mentality. Would anyone "use" their beloved? Use their child? Use their friend? If we, being human, know these things, how much more would our Father, who is Love Himself, use us? When we use the word *used*, I believe we are missing something key.

God saved you because He loves you and longs to restore your relationship. You were rescued and redeemed to be with God, the One who delights in you, yearns to walk with you, to enjoy your presence, to see you become fully human, fully alive, fully your own self.

God does not want to use you: God wants to be with you because He loves you.

There's the hint in His name itself: Immanuel. His very name is *God with us*. Not God to us. Not God using us. Not God for us. Not God managing us. Not God working us. Not God manipulating or puppeteering us. He tipped His own hand right there in Isaiah with the word about the Word—He is God with us.

> *God does not want to use you: God wants to be with you because He loves you.*

We aren't being used by God. See the difference there? We are walking *with* God, holding His hand, in step wherever we go, whatever we do—"important" or not.

In my current vocabulary, I've replaced the word *use* with the verbs and nouns of the New Testament: grow, disciple, walk in the way, beloved children, co-heirs, co-laborers. And don't forget, now: *Jesus called us friends.*

Friend of God. Child of God. Beloved of God.

Taste and see: we are invited to the God-with-us life. In co-creation with the Creator, you're a namer, a maker, an altar builder, a lifter-up of the name and the Cross, and you are a pilgrim, a disciple, made in the image of God; you are the one who walks with God without shame.

So those things we do in this life? Great. Wonderful. Good on us.

But I'm learning to just go and do them simply because I love to do them and I love to do them with Immanuel. I'm learning to let them be the natural consequences of the sacred company I keep, but those things aren't my identity. They're not my pathway to God, or my status updates to the Most High, my progress reports, my way of proving my gratitude. I'm co-creating with God in my life, and it all matters—from the visible to the hidden.

When we love God, when we are free, when we are walking with, *then we are a sign and a foretaste of how it was meant to be in the Garden.*

May our daily work and our voice and our words and our prayers matter in our homes and our churches and our neighborhoods (right there is the whole world). But we are not simply "used"—not like that. Instead, when we love God, when we are free, when we are walking *with*, then we are a sign and a foretaste of how it was meant to be in the Garden, perhaps. And God's way of living can overflow organically in the disciple, the friend, the daughter, the son, the brother, the sister, the heir, the beloved.

* * *

Christianity sees the whole entire world as God's and as headed toward redemption. When we stop seeing ourselves as used and begin seeing ourselves as invited to participate as co-creators and partners in every corner of our humanity, then all our life can be set aflame with the presence of God. Paul says in Colossians 1:15–19:

> We look at this Son and see God's original purpose in everything created. For everything, absolutely everything, above and below, visible and invisible, rank after rank after rank of angels—*everything* got started in Him and finds its purpose in Him. He was there before any of it came into existence and holds it all together right up to this moment. And when it comes to the Church, He organizes and holds it together, like a head does a body. He was supreme in the beginning and—leading the resurrection parade—He is supreme in the end. From beginning to end He's there, towering far above everything, everyone. So spacious is He, so roomy, that everything of God finds its proper place in Him without crowding. Not only that, but all the broken and dislocated pieces of the universe—people and things, animals and atoms—get properly fixed and fit together in vibrant harmonies, all

222 Out of Sorts

because of His death, His blood that poured down from the cross.

What else is there to say?

* * *

One part of our evangelical hero complex that I was happy to leave behind was the exhaustion. Gracious, it's tiring, isn't it? I wasn't just physically tired of carrying the weight of the world on my shoulders. I was tired of feeling like I didn't measure up. Tired of feeling inconsequential. Tired of defining success by what others could quantify in terms of numbers. Tired of ignoring the foster parents, the hospice workers, the carpenters, the writers, the teachers, the prophets disguised as mothers. And especially tired of feeling like it all—whatever it was—depended on me.

For me, it was a subtle shift but a powerful one. Instead of becoming someone who "did" things, I simply took my place in my own life as it is now. Instead of waiting for some mythical "there" of ministry, I could simply live as if my life were ministry. Instead of trying harder to be more loving, I learned simply to love. Richard Rohr writes this: "You do not 'do' acts of peace and justice as much as your life is *itself* peace and justice. You take your small and sufficient place in the great and grand scheme of God."[9] The Kingdom of God starts small, a grain of wheat, a mustard seed, leaven in the loaf. And it spreads, oh, yes, it grows. But it starts small, hidden in the secret places. Jesus told us stories of candles on a lamp stand and small lights that can't be hidden.

Now, I've learned—and I am learning—to respect and celebrate the work of all of us, the people of God. Like Paul, "pray that our God will make you fit for what He's called you to be, pray that he'll fill your good ideas and acts of faith with His own energy so that it all amounts to something." [10] We serve the God Who Sees, and I want to see with those eyes.

Even those people doing the big traditionally evangelical hero things have told me that they are just doing one thing at a time, and the daily work of it doesn't feel or look that sexy. There is a lot of blood, sweat, and small wins coupled with small failures. For instance, someone once told me that being a writer and a preacher is such an amazing thing to do, but it doesn't feel amazing. It feels like a lot of work, a lot of days spent at the public library tapping on an old laptop covered in sticky fingerprints from the tinies doing homework. It feels like writing during nap time and editing while nursing a newborn. It feels like studying and learning and working theology out into my real life. It feels like an aspect of what I do every day while I show up in my whole life with intention and God takes the entire sum of it and makes something beautiful out of it. But it's not heroic, not really. It's a vocation. It is the work God gave me to do.

One soul is as valuable as thousands, millions. One soul is as important as ninety-nine. One soul is worth leaving behind everything to rescue. If there is one soul in your care, one face in your loving gaze, one hand you are holding, then you are holding the world. The work you do today, the love you give and receive and lavish on the seemingly small people and tasks— all of these "little" things tip the scales of justice and mercy in our world. Everything we do, from the mundane to the glamorous to the difficult and all points between, can testify.

* * *

Eventually, the opportunity arose for us to pastor a church again. It was entirely my fault that we learned about it. Since leaving ministry, Brian has reinvented himself—first as a carpenter and eventually working his way through the ranks to become a general manager for a restoration company. But every once in a while, I would still check ministry postings at certain websites without telling him. I thought he wanted to return to ministry at some point. On this particular day I found a posting for what looked to be his dream job: a small to mid-size church within our faith tradition and—and here's the kicker—it was near his hometown.

Well, of course he applied for the job with my full support. We went through all the rounds of interviews and it was going beautifully. Brian was perfectly qualified, and he seemed like a dream fit for the community in terms of personality, ministry philosophy, and so on. On paper, everything made sense.

And yet.

Something didn't feel right. It wasn't just that I didn't want to move, but I'll be straight honest and say that no, I did not want to move. We live less than ten minutes from my parents, to whom we are very close. My sister and her little family live just down the hill from my parents. She is my very best friend and has been for our entire life together. Our little gaggle of tinies don't know the difference between cousins and siblings. Adding to the complication was the fact that I love everything about British Columbia: it feels like my soul-home. We're caught here on the edge of the wilderness between the mountains and the ocean. This was the place where I found God in new and unexpected ways, the location of my rebirth, my origin for any theology of place that I've developed in my life so far. I have wanted to stay here forever, to put down roots, and practice the radical act of faith that is known as simply staying put. But I told Brian that I would lay all of that down on the altar if he wanted to go. Ministry first, I defaulted.

In years past, when opportunities to reenter full-time vocational ministry had arisen, he had backed away, knowing that I wasn't ready for that kind of life again. He loved me more than he loved being in ministry. I had never forgotten that. I would never forget. So this time around, I wanted whatever we did here to be his decision. I wasn't going to hold him back. I trusted the Holy Spirit's leading in his life. If he ended up saying no to this opportunity, it had to be because he felt led in that direction, not out of worry for me or acquiescence to my fears. I was fine. I could do this.

It was his turn to choose, and I knew that this one had to be his choice. I thought back to that time at the beginning of our marriage when I had laid down my career dreams for his call to ministry, and I wondered if this would be a decade-later repeat of that decision. Perhaps we had always been headed to this choice again.

Brian wrestled over that entire summer. On one hand, he was excited. He longed to spend his days doing work for which he had been trained and educated, work to which he had once felt called. But as the summer wore on, something began to rise up between us. I tried to name it and figure it out. I felt like Brian was . . . afraid. His conversation that summer turned into the scarcity-laden words of "What if this is it? What if this is my one chance? What if I say no and I never have another opportunity to pastor?"

We don't resolve everything at the moment of crisis. Some resolutions have to be lived into. This was one of those for us.

We don't resolve everything at the moment of crisis.

But one night, I laid everything on the table and confessed that I was terrified he was going to turn our entire lives upside down because he was somehow afraid his life as it stood was not enough, not because he was called. He had bought into a narrative of scarcity instead of a narrative of abundance.

Few theologians have influenced me the way that Walter Brueggemann has—perhaps N. T. Wright and Dallas Willard are up there with him—from my political and economic engagement to my vocation as a writer to even my personal discipleship. His work on the "liturgy of abundance" versus the "myth of scarcity"[11] is primarily for the big picture—the empire, economics, justice for the poor, war—but because I am one woman with a fairly small life and realm of influence, I find that his words illuminated even here in the individual and communal ways.

The myth of scarcity tells the powerful to accumulate and take and dominate, to be driven by the fear of not enough and never enough. We make our decisions out of a fear that there isn't enough for us. These core beliefs can lead us to the treacheries of war and hunger, injustice and inequality. We think we must keep others down so we can stay on top. We stockpile money and food and comforts at the expense of one another and our own souls. Throughout Scripture, we see the impact of the myth of scarcity on—and even within—the nation of Israel. The prophets wrote and stood in bold criticism against those who—out of the fear of not enough—built their empire on the backs of the poor and oppressed.

But the Kingdom of God is more than enough. It is an act of faith to live with the narrative of abundance instead of the fear of scarcity.

It is an act of faith to live with the narrative of abundance instead of the fear of scarcity.

As the Church, we are called to exist in a prophetic community, an alternative to the narratives of the world, living out the Kingdom of God in our right-now lives. There isn't scarcity. There is more than enough in Christ.

Scarcity tells us to work until we drop. We've got to hustle, hustle, hustle to get ours and then to keep it. But in the liturgy of abundance, we can practice Sabbath. Exhaustion and burn-out are symptoms of our fear of scarcity, but wholeness, joy, and rest are hallmarks of a life lived within abundance. In fact, Brueggemann calls the practice of Sabbath an act of resistance because we are saying no to "the culture of now."[12]

But it's within the life of our Jesus that we see it most clearly: Jesus was the full embodiment of what it means to be human in the way God intended. He uplifts instead of tearing down, He heals instead of wounds, He lays down His life instead of fighting to survive, He chooses compassion instead of numb acceptance, He is water to a thirsty soul, bread to the hungry, oil of joy for mourning. And instead of death, He is life. Life!

Jesus was the full embodiment of what it means to be human in the way God intended.

There is more than enough for us all, there is room for us all, and everything that Love intends for us to become will come to fruition in the appointed time.

* * *

Brian was stunned by my challenge that night in our living room. We had a long night of discussion while the tinies slept. And during that night, the truth came out: Brian was experiencing the last dying gasp of our evangelical hero complex.

Even though we knew better, even though he thought he had resolved every last remnant of division and dualism, of the false gospel of secular work versus sacred work, he still found himself feeling the pull toward full-time vocational ministry, not out of a clear sense of calling or direction, but out of the fear that his life was not enough. He felt like a failure because he wasn't in ministry anymore. He missed feeling like a hero.

We didn't resolve much that night. But we talked about it, and we named it for what it was: fear.

It was the fear of missing out, the fear of being not enough, the fear of disappointing God, and even of disappointing other people. It was the fear of finally embracing a life different for yourself than the one you had been given at the beginning. Brian had spent twenty-five years preparing for ministry. Up until now, we had seen this season of our life as "a break" from ministry: it wasn't forever, and it wasn't really on purpose. It was just how life had gone. He had forged a whole new career—and a whole new self—in the meantime. But if he walked away from this opportunity—so seemingly perfect on paper—was he in essence actually walking away from his calling? Was he closing the door once and forever on full-time vocational ministry?

He felt like a failure because he wasn't in ministry anymore. He missed feeling like a hero.

Even as my understanding of calling and vocation has shifted and changed over the years, I still hold on to the idea of work as an honorable thing, that our vocations can be tied to the plans and purposes of God. I hold on to the belief that we each do work that makes us feel more alive and connected to God. For me, it's writing. For my husband, it's carpentry, leading, and teaching.

I have found that we still walk in those anointings, even without job titles and salaries to accompany them. After all, Brian and I live in a context now that doesn't brag of many megachurches. The large rosters of full-time pastors don't exist in our world. For instance, at our church, there is a full-time lead pastor, but the other people who are on staff often serve bivocationally, meaning that they work another job half or even three-quarters of the time because there simply isn't a full-time salary available. This is life in a post-Christian context or in a context that doesn't boast large tax returns.

I hope the Church continues to move toward missional embodiment, the theology of place, incarnational ministry, and embracing the value of how our everyday lives can embody the Gospel in very essential ways. In this new emergence, I see us as a people moving from the "in front" to the "beside," and I couldn't be happier about it. I think it's healthier all the way around—for the Church, for the leadership, for the world. The less hero worship, the less celebrity, the fewer big-name camps, the fewer video venues and names in lights, the better off the Church.

The less hero worship, the less celebrity, the fewer big-name camps, the fewer video venues and names in lights, the better off the Church.

I may be tipping my cards a bit here: I don't mind the little ways. I find God in the ordinary quotidian rhythms of my life,

I do. Breaking bread and pouring wine happens in my living room. Few things restore my soul like ordinary work—cleaning, walking, cooking. The real transformations of my life didn't come about at a conference or a Sunday morning service or during a mountaintop moment; the real transformations in my spirit and my character and my life were born and tended and raised in the daily mundane habits and faithfulness of my life.

The real transformations in my spirit and my character and my life were born and tended and raised in the daily mundane habits and faithfulness of my life.

I like the idea of being planted in the house of God, of putting one's roots down into a community and remaining there. Church gatherings work best when they connect me to my real life, where I actually live out the hope of glory.

I've learned to reimagine ministry. I worry that our evangelical hero complexes are fracturing the Body of Christ. That they are making us go from experience to experience, stadium to stadium, round table to panel, think tank to gathering, instead of burrowing down into our real lives and leading well, right where God has placed us.

I don't see a lot of marketing language in the New Testament. Not a lot of strategizing and branding, not a lot of business planning or factory farming, not a lot of Discipleship-O-Matic or Identi-Kit churches. Instead, I see relationship, I see intimacy, I see organic growth. I see making disciples one by one by one by one. I see the little ways.

So how do we include the rest of us in these conversations about vocation and calling? How do we make room and open the doors for those of us who do good work outside the church context? Particularly those of us who are sick and housebound or in a difficult season of life? Those who are single parents and don't have someone else at home handling things? Those who are global? Those who are poor or working-class or living paycheck to paycheck? Those who are outside our usual narrative and profile of leadership? The ones who aren't perceived as good-looking and influential?

I believe all of our lives are a proclamation. I preach sometimes these days, sure, but that's not my identity. I don't even find my identity in being a writer. I am instead God's beloved one, just as you are, and my desire isn't for a particular title but instead

I believe all of our lives are a proclamation.

to walk wherever He walks and follow the scent of His presence, to discern where Jesus is moving and move there. And of course I want to keep telling stories about all the ways I see and experience and know His goodness in the world. Sometimes that looks like preaching on Sunday morning, sometimes that looks like blogging or writing a book, sometimes that looks like advocating for justice at home or in Haiti, sometimes that looks like bathing my babies and tucking money under a little girl's pillow with a note from the tooth fairy, before I crawl back into bed with my husband.

* * *

One day, I came home and Brian told me that he had removed himself as a candidate for that ministry job. It was not an easy decision to make, but it was the right thing to do. He couldn't make a life-changing decision out of fear of being not enough. It wasn't fair to us, and it wouldn't be fair to the community of people just wanting a pastor, for heaven's sake.

And just as some moments that we think will be huge in our lives turn out to be little more than a blip on the radar, this seemingly small decision brought unforeseen consequences of freedom and renewal in our lives.

We were free.

Free to work to the glory of God, no matter whether my husband found himself on a job site or in a church. We look back now at that moment, and I can actually see Him as He became lighter, more grounded in his everyday life, instead of following the alternative storyline of narrow definitions of ministry or a "life worth living." As E. M. Forster wrote, we were finally able to let go of the life we had planned, in order to have the life that was waiting for us.

The heavy burdens of our evangelical hero complex, our identity, our questions of worth and being used by God, all of it—in that moment, we surrendered them. We laid them down on the altar, set them on fire, and stood back at last. They burned down to ashes before our eyes, and yes, some younger version of ourselves ached with the loss of it. But the exhaustion disappeared, the feelings of worthlessness, the crippling misidentity went up in smoke.

Now, when we speak of feeling called, we speak of feeling called to the life we have right now.

We were free of them at last. And that meant we were free to live into our right-now lives with intention and purpose. Now, when we speak of feeling called, we speak of feeling called to the life we have right now. This is our work. This is our vocation. This is our calling. This little family, each other, our community, our work—both of us, our preaching, our teaching, our labor, our play, all the millions of small ways our imperfect candle is up on the lamp stand, blazing bright enough for us. Immanuel, God with us.

Benediction

*

You and I are sitting in a mess of half-unpacked boxes, aren't we? We have a few piles here and there. This looks like a home-made altar to me.

I know that the idea of wilderness is sometimes romanticized in literature or sermons by the now-clean and tidy prosperous ones who wax philosophic about rediscovery. But there's nothing romantic about the arduous task of sorting through a lifetime of questions and wonderings. We sort on the threshold of grief and change, it's a liminal space, and I hope you know I'm just as dirty and disheveled as everyone else. Because we never stop.

You'll set out on this journey with your trunks and baggage, boxes and piles in tow. And if you're anything like me, you might feel a bit of smugness: I was certain I would arrive on the other side with my pet gods firmly intact. But as the journey carries on, you will leave a trail behind you, a littering of the contents of your baggage, and slowly—sometimes bitterly, it must be admitted—your walk through the wilderness will become unencumbered. You may sit by the trail and cry over the poisonous, lovely things being left behind. You'll wonder why you're still holding on to this thing or that thing. You'll find that some things you were ready to toss have become dear, so precious, that you'll carry them in your lap to keep them safe.

But every single one of those items you leave along the trail—your cynicism, your hypocrisy, your lies, your numbing techniques, your apologetics and doctrinal statements, your worldview, your pomposity, your opinions, your carefully constructed personas, your sins, your righteousness, your secrets—all of it will become filthy rags, and in the end, you will be nearly flinging them off the wagon, glad to be rid of them at last, I promise.

When you find streams in the desert, the hands of those who love the Gospel will be the ones who hand you just enough water to drink. You will swallow the dust down with the cool water and cry with relief before setting out again.

No, the wilderness isn't romantic, but it's beautiful and terrifying and intimate. Eventually, there won't be anything between you and God anymore. There is freedom and deliverance waiting on the other side; sometimes it won't look the way the travel brochure sold it, though. You'll look back from your new home in the west, and you'll love the wind and the wild, you'll love your freckles and the sun's slow weathering of your bare face. You'll love the song of the stars in your hair more than you loved the contents of your life, more than you loved tidy sealed boxes and certainty.

You'll love the song of the stars in your hair more than you loved the contents of your life, more than you loved tidy sealed boxes and certainty.

And here's the secret: you will still feel the call in the wind, beckoning you further west. You'll face the prospect of another journey and the likelihood of another one on the other side of that, and some part of you will look forward to the nights alone on the prairie when the voice of God sings clear in your bones. You'll pack up for the new journey, another betwixt-and-between, another adventure in sorting it all out, and you'll wonder which of these essential and important things will litter the new trail ahead of you. You're a pioneer, an explorer, an adventurer: carry on.

I need to pray for you and with you and over you. Fair warning: the way I pray may not be the way you pray, and that's okay. That's part of the beauty of it.

So first, let me do this: Beloved one, I pray you won't be afraid.

I pray for bravery and guts, for honesty and discernment. I know you have a lot to lose—we all do when we lay down our certainties and our black-and-white thinking. It's terrifying to grow up, if you really think about it. But the Lord is your light and your salvation, whom shall you fear? The Lord is the stronghold of your life, of whom should you be afraid? (Psalm 27:1). I pray that when people, often well-meaning, try to quiet your questions or placate you or numb you, you would remember that God has not given you a spirit of fear but a spirit of love and power and a sound mind (2 Timothy 1:7).

I pray you would remember that God is not threatened by you and that the slippery slope may very well be your saving grace, sending you careening into truth and love, newness and beauty. There is no fear in love. But perfect love drives out fear, because fear has to do with punishment. The one who fears is

not made perfect in love (1 John 4:18). Fear is not our motiva-
tor. Fear is not our address. Fear is not our ruler. We are *not* a
people of fear but a people of love.

I pray you would come to know Jesus, deeply and intimately.
I pray you would fall in step with the man from Nazareth and
that His way of life would become life for you—life more abundant. I pray you would have your ideas of Jesus, your precon-
ceptions, your thought-I-knew-Him disrupted. I pray you would
find yourself apprenticed to Him in all ways. I pray for you to
love Him, yes, to love Jesus and the Father and Spirit to whom
He introduced us, with all your heart and all your mind and
all your soul. I pray that He would be your first and your last.

I pray that you would embrace your place in the Body of Christ, your right to learn and test, your right to read and explore.

I pray you would embrace your
place in the Body of Christ, your
right to learn and test, your right
to read and explore. I know that
sometimes it seems as if there is
more room for wonder and delight,
beauty and mystery and grandeur
in astrophysics than there is in religion. That's because religion
tells us that it's all figured out, there is nothing left to learn,
here are the answers, so learn them. But instead, I pray you
would be an explorer, you would recover delight and wonder
and curiosity about your faith, about God, and about the story
with which you continue to wrestle.

I pray that the Bible would capture your imagination and
heart again. I pray that you would read these sacred words with
new eyes and a heart to receive. I come against any abuse that
you may have endured in the name of Scripture or any ways
that the story of God has been used against you. I pray for healing in those wounds. I pray for eyes to see and ears to hear what

the Spirit is saying to you. I pray that your soul would hunger for Scripture and for prayer, I pray that the words of the Bible would become your great anthem, your comfort, and your place of belonging. May Scripture shape your prayers with stories and truth, promises and declarations, poems and metaphors. Reading the Bible is still the best way I can think of to listen: what is the Spirit saying to you? May your life be an overflow of the Story. May Scripture change your life, change your tongue, change your mind, and so change the world. But be ready to be wrong about a few things first.

I pray for you as a beloved member of the Church. Yes, you, you are a beloved member of the Church, you are part of the Body; we wouldn't be us without you. We need you and your voice, your experience and your wisdom. We need your talents and your failures. I pray for you to find your place, whether it's an official four-walls-and-a-tax-status gathering or a home-made mismatch of misfits in a basement. I pray for friendship and community to become a source of life for you. I pray that when you are lonely, you would find your family. May you come alive in relationship while still keeping the spark of you burning, no homogeny but beautiful diversity. I pray that you would create what you are craving be-cause chances are you aren't alone *I pray for the real to show* even if you think you are. I pray for *up in the Body of Christ.* a small handful of Somewheres, not too many of course, just the few, to know you at your best and your worst, for you to love them and show up for them and be their person. I pray for authenticity and realness, for the shedding of masks and expectations. I pray for the real to show up in the Body of Christ. I pray you would learn how to cham-pion and celebrate others, to put others first. This is not time for pettiness and who-is-in-and-who-is-out. We're all in. May you make time for fun and for joy, to be silly and go on adventures.

I pray for you to embrace your place in the Kingdom of God. I pray that you would have your eyes opened—look! It's already here! You're part of it and so am I. Anywhere and everywhere that we are, as the people of God, we are proclaiming and establishing the Kingdom of God. You may feel like an exile— that's because you kind of are. Plant gardens in your exile, work for the good of the city, and don't be so caught up in the "not yet" of the Kingdom of God that you forget it's also now.

I pray that you would know that you are a part of something bigger than yourself, that you would be able to look back and look around to see that you are part of a big and glorious story, a big messy rummage sale that's been going on for millennia. I pray that when you don't have words, the words of those pilgrims before you would find their way to your mouth. I pray that when you find yourself in Pentecost or Epiphany, Christmas or ordinary time, you would feel connected to the story of God instead of the marketing calendar of a card company. I pray that you would feel anchored, like you're part of a family, a tradition, a practice. I pray for your memory to strengthen, that the Spirit would make sense of the line of time that stretches backward from you and your time and includes the great cloud of witnesses.

I pray for the active and intimate leading of the Holy Spirit. Oh, yes, I'm going there. I pray for signs and wonders, for dreams and visions, for miracles and intimacy. I pray for an open mind and an open heart: I pray that you would hear what the Spirit is saying to the Church. May you walk in an awareness of the Spirit, in the comfort and company and conviction. I pray for Spirit-led boldness and gentleness. I pray that you would bear the fruit of the Spirit in your life as you abide in the Vine of Christ. May you become a person of love, joy, peace, patience, kindness, goodness, faithfulness, gentleness, and self-control. May you be perfumed with the scent of heaven and may you be a thorn in the side of the enemy. I pray that you would honor your hunger and your thirst. Don't outsource the work of the Holy Spirit in your life to someone else.

I pray that when you are grieving and suffering, you would find peace and wholeness again. God isn't to blame. I really believe that; may that truth comfort you. I pray for you to feel held and carried in your time of great need, because it will come if it hasn't already. You have a voice for lament as well as for praise. Cry out to God.

I pray for your heart to be broken and your anger to be woken up. I come against anything that would try to separate your gospel from your feet and your hands and your habits and your money. I pray that your everyday life would become an outpost for justice to roll down. I pray for perseverance and renewal, for the dry places to bloom with flowers, for the mountains to bow down and the valleys to rise up. I pray that you would be a learner, a listener, and a humble worker. I pray that as you push back the darkness,

I pray that your everyday life would become an outpost for justice to roll down.

painful step by step, that you would be empowered by the Spirit for mighty deeds. I pray for courage and for perseverance and humility.

As we rise from a world, a culture, a past that is shouting lies about our very created and called selves, oh, Almighty One, sweep the entanglements of our sin and those lies from our souls. Show us that our fetter is but a spiderweb compared to the fury of your freedom sweeping in, the wonder of your wide-open door and fresh air.

The battle is yours, and it is won, as Jesus said: we can put our swords back where they belong. We belong to you, we belong to the family of God. We are named, we are loved, we call each other by our real names. May we lift up our heads from the despair and find the family we have always yearned to find.

May we be ones who speak the words of Paul in Ephesians 2:19–22 to one another:

> That's plain enough, isn't it? You're no longer wandering exiles. This kingdom of faith is now your home country. You're no longer strangers or outsiders. You belong here, with as much right to the name Christian as anyone. God is building a home. . . . We see it taking shape day after day—a holy temple built by God, all of us built into it, a temple in which God is quite at home.

May we be the ones who don't give up on radical inclusion. May we remember to whisper to one another, every now and then, on purpose, at the right time: You belong here. There's room for you. There's room for all of us. We are part of the temple in which God is quite at home.

Patience and faith belong together. May you remember that you have so much to learn and treat the people in your life as your teachers. Everything you do in your life can be a testimony to the goodness and freedom and openness of our God.

May we be the ones who hold the doors open for others, who hold hands, who hold faces, who hold secrets for one another, who hold space for the pain and the brilliance, who hold the light and the salt, the complexity and the simplicity, the silence and the storm, the ones who hold our opinions loosely and yet love ferociously.

Everything you do is Spirit-filled if you intend it to be. There isn't a hero in the kingdom; we are all beginners. Remember the ones who lead you are also on the ground, not on a pedestal. We will fail you in some way. I wish that weren't true but it is: give us grace, please.

I pray for your vocation and your calling. Oh, may your hands find the work you were meant to do. I pray that wherever you find yourself—on a stage or in a position of influence or perhaps your kitchen table or beautiful obscurity—you would find God in all the days of your life, in all the callings, in all the places. I pray for the holy to invade you daily. I pray that your eyes and heart would be open to see where God is hiding in plain sight. Instead of waiting for your real life to start, I call you to wake up! Wake up! Your life is happening, this is where God has placed you. May you become a parable of hope and renewal right where you are.

And here, at the last, as we sit here among the questions still unanswered and the path you must walk ahead, I pray for your journey as it unfolds into the unknown.

I know you feel a bit out of sorts. We all do sometimes. It's okay. Don't be afraid.

You are so very loved. I pray you would remember it, know it, live it, breathe it, rest in it: beloved.

In the mighty and the powerful name of Jesus,
Amen.

Sarah Bessey
Epiphany 2015

Garage Sale for Orphans

✳

If you would like to do a bit of real-life sorting with an eye on doing a bit of good, please check out Garage Sale for Orphans with Help One Now. All your excess stuff could contribute to ending the cycle of extreme poverty.

Here's what you do:

1. Plan your garage sale.
2. Share the vision with your neighborhood or church.
3. Host your garage sale. Go ahead and throw a party for the neighborhood.
4. When you're all done, send the money you've made to Help One Now to support our work in Haiti or Zimbabwe, Peru, or Uganda.

For more information and resources, tips and ideas, check out: https://www.helponenow.org/garage-sale-for-orphans/.

Thank You

*

Thank you to my husband, Brian. I love you and I am proud of you. In all the beautiful loud crazy of our life, you're the one and you'll always be the one. This book wouldn't have been written without your constant and unwavering belief that my work matters. MTB. Thank you to our tinies: Anne, Joe, Evelynn Joan, and Maggie Love. I could eat you up, I love you so. Thank you to my parents, David and Joan Styles, for empowering me to own both my story and my search, and for being the best and truest example I could fathom of a man and woman after God's own heart. Thank you to my sister and lobster, Amanda, for being my first and best and faithful Somewhere. Thank you to my in-laws for all their support, particularly my mother-in-law, Leona. Thank you to Sally for being so much more than a two-day-a-week babysitter; you're part of our family, and I can't imagine how this would have gotten done without you. Thank you to the churches of my life, past and present, for your grace as I wrestled these words out in our very real lives. Thank you to the readers of *Jesus Feminist* and to the community at sarahbessey.com who have prayed and questioned this book into existence. Your e-mails, notes, messages, stories, celebrations, criticisms, and tweets matter more than you could know. Thank you to my friends, my Somewheres, my sisterhood, my secret society, my writing room, my tribe, and my community—you know who you are to me, and you know I wouldn't have survived writing this book in this season of my life without your practical help, prayer, laughter, and commitment. A particular thank you to Nish, Amber, Megan, Laura, Kelley, Jen, Kristen, Tara, Sarah, Jamie, and Glennon. Thank you to Kevin, Rachelle, and Michaela along with your families for carrying on so beautifully. Thank you to Austin Brown for her advice at a key point in this book. Thank you to the team and partners and friends at Help One Now for wrecking my life so beautifully. Thank you to my literary agent, Rachelle Gardner, along with the team at Books & Such. Thank you to my booking agent, Jim Chaffee, for connecting me with real-life people. Thank you to the entire team at Howard Books, particularly Philis Boultinghouse.

And finally, always, only Jesus. Still, forever, nothing compares to you. Even now, I am still singing of how your name is like honey on my lips.

Notes

✳

CHAPTER ONE: OUT OF SORTS

1. Emily Dickinson, "Tell all the truth but tell it slant" from *The Poems of Emily Dickinson: Reading Edition*, ed. by Ralph W. Franklin (Cambridge: Belknap Press, 1998).
2. Kierkegaard wrote this in an entry in his *Papers and Journals* in 1843.
3. Paul Ricoeur, *The Symbolism of Evil* (Boston: Beacon Press, 1967), 349.
4. Richard Rohr, *Falling Upward: A Spirituality for the Two Halves of Life* (San Francisco: Jossey-Bass, 2011), 60.
5. Phyllis Tickle, *The Great Emergence: How Christianity is Changing and Why* (Grand Rapids: Baker Books, 2012), 17.
6. William Sears and Martha Sears, *The Birth Book: Everything You Need to Know to Have a Safe and Satisfying Birth* (New York: Little, Brown, 1994), 134.

CHAPTER TWO: THERE'S SOMETHING ABOUT THAT NAME

1. Bill Gaither and Gloria Gaither, "There's Something About That Name," (Spring House Music Group: 1970).
2. *Bullfrogs and Butterflies: God Is My Friend* (Burlington, VT: Birdwing Records), 1978.
3. Mary Oliver, "The Journey," *New and Selected Poems*, vol. 1 (Boston: Beacon Press, 2004).

4. "Romans Road" lays out a plan of salvation using Bible verses from the Book of Romans. It was considered an easy and systemic method of explaining to a potential convert who needs to be saved, what it means to be saved, and why it is necessary. When I was a kid, there were cheat sheets available to fit in one's wallet with the Bible verses so that one would never be caught without a clear plan of salvation for the curious.

5. Martin J. Nystrom, "As the Deer," 1981, as recorded by Maranatha! Singers.

6. Brennan Manning, *The Relentless Tenderness of Jesus* (Ada, MI: Revell, 2004), 20.

7. Greg Boyd, *Is God to Blame?* (Downers Grove, IL: IVP Books, 2003), 39.

8. Psalm 42:7.

9. Matthew 20:1–16.

10. Rev. 1:5.

11. John 14:2.

12. Brennan Manning, *Relentless Tenderness*, 121.

13. 1 Corinthians 10:17 MSG.

14. Richard Rohr, *Eager to Love* (Cincinnati: Franciscan Media, 2014), 9.

15. Keith Green, "Oh Lord, You're Beautiful," (Nashville: Universal Music Publishing Group, 1980).

CHAPTER THREE: EVERYONE GETS TO PLAY

1. Robert Farrar Capon, *The Supper of the Lamb* (New York: Doubleday, 1969).

2. John Wimber, *"Everyone Gets to Play"* (Garden City, ID: Ampelon Publishing, 2008).

3. This phrase originates in a story of Jesus in Matthew 18:3 (NIV): "He called a little child to Him, and placed the child among them. And He said: "'Truly I tell you, unless you change and become like little children, you will never enter the kingdom of heaven. Therefore, whoever takes the lowly position of this child is the greatest in the kingdom of heaven. And whoever welcomes one such child in my name welcomes me.'"

4. Psalm 139:9.

5. James W. Fowler, *Stages of Faith: The Psychology of Human Development and the Quest for Meaning"* (New York: HarperCollins, 1981, 1995).

6. Ibid., 164.
7. *Their Eyes Were Watching God* (New York: Harper Perennial Modern Classics, 2006).
8. John 6:68.

CHAPTER FOUR: GETTING INTO THE WORD

1. John 1:16–18.
2. Peter Enns, *For the Bible Tells Me So: Why Defending Scripture Has Made Us Unable to Read It* (San Francisco: HarperOne, 2014), 8.
3. Ibid., 61
4. http://ntwrightpage.com/Wright_Bible_Authoritative.htm.
6. This references 2 Corinthians 4:7 and is inspired by a similar meditation by Marcus Borg.
6. Enns, 63.
7. Ibid., 170.
8. Matthew 5:38–44 NIV.
9. John 5:39–40 NLT.
10. http://brianzahnd.com/2014/01/scripture-witness-word-god/.
11. Galatians 3:28.
12. I came across this phrase in the work of American liberation theologian Gustavo Gutiérrez.
13. Brian McLaren, "The Problem Isn't the Bible," blog post on Patheos, June 18, 2014.
    http://www.patheos.com/Topics/2014–Religious-Trends/Progressive-Christian/The-Problem-Isnt-the-Bible-Brian-McLaren-06182014?offset=1&max=1.

CHAPTER FIVE: THE PEOPLE OF GOD

1. Jonathan Martin, *Prototype* (Carol Stream, IL: Tyndale, 2013), 80.
2. Darrell Guder, ed., *The Missional Church* (Grand Rapids, MI: Eardmans, 1998), 4.
3. Jürgen Moltmann in David J. Bosch, *Transforming Mission: Paradigm Shifts in Theology of Mission* (Maryknoll, NY: Orbis Books, 2011), 390. As Bosch continues, "Mission is thereby seen as a movement from God to the world; the Church is viewed as an instrument for that mission."
4. "Mission is not primarily an activity of the church, but an attribute of God." Bosch, 390.

5. John 20:21.
6. Acts 1:8.
7. Dr. Ross W. Hastings, "Theological and Missional Themes in the Book of Acts" (lecture taught for Application 610: Empowering the Church for First World Re-Evangelization), Regent College, Vancouver, January 17, 2007.
8. Miroslav Volf, *After Our Likeness: The Church as the Image of the Trinity* (Grand Rapids, MI: Eerdmans, 1998), 234.
9. Ibid.
10. Ibid., 235.
11. Charles Ringma, *Catch the Wind: A Precursor to the Emergent Church* (Sutherland, NSW: Albatross, 1994), 71.
12. "It is God's prerogative to maintain the essence of the Church; it is our responsibility to make sure that the structures we create reflect the heart of God's intention for His people." Ringma, 73.
13. This is also what Van Engen is getting at: church leaders should "move the congregation to create plans, make decisions, and resolve internal conflicts always with the objective of mobilizing God's missionary people." Charles Van Engen, *God's Missionary People: Rethinking the Purpose of the Local Church* (Grand Rapids, MI: Baker, 1991), 186.
14. Jacques Ellul, *The Presence of the Kingdom* (Colorado Springs: Helmers & Howard, 1989), 80.
15. "One of the most important tangible forms of that conversion is the Church's willingness to change its visible structures in order to become more faithful to it mission." Guder, 231
16. Ibid., 230.
17. Van Engen, 191.
18. Ringma, 73–74.

CHAPTER SIX: BE A PERSON

1. Shane Claiborne, Jonathan Wilson-Hartgrove, and Enuma Okoro, *Common Prayer: A Liturgy for Ordinary Radicals* (Grand Rapids, MI: Zondervan, 2010), 564.
2. Jean Vanier, *Community and Growth* (Mahwah, NJ: Paulist Press, 1989), 310.
3. Brené Brown, *The Gifts of Imperfection: Let Go of Who You Think You're Supposed to Be and Embrace Who You Are* (Center City, MN: Hazelden, 2010), 11.

4. This idea is based on Rick Warren's circles of church leadership/ membership (congregation, community, core) in *The Purpose Driven Church: Growth Without Compromising Your Message and Mission* (Grand Rapids, MI: Zondervan, 1995), 129.
5. Henri Nouwen, *Intimacy* (Nashville, TN: HarperOne, 2009), 23.
6. Dietrich Bonhoeffer, *Life Together: Prayerbook of the Bible* (Minneapolis, MN: Fortress Press, 1996), 34.
7. Kurt Vonnegut, *Palm Sunday: An Autobiographical Collage* (New York: Dial Press Trade Paperback, 1999), 180.

CHAPTER SEVEN: TRULY HUMAN

1. Psalm 126:1–3.
2. Henry David Thoreau wrote in *Walden*: "The mass of men live lives of quiet desperation."
3. Interview with Keith Giles, http://www.dwillard.org/articles/artview .asp?artID=150.
4. Dallas Willard, *The Divine Conspiracy: Rediscovering Our Hidden Life in God* (New York: Harper, 1998), 94–95
5. John 10:10.
6. Jonathan Merritt, "The Bible Term Most misused by Christians Today: An Interview with Scot McKnight," *Religion News Service*, October 15, 2014.
7. Brennan Manning, *The Furious Longing of God* (Colorado Springs: David C. Cook, 2009), 125.
8. Luke 4:17–21, *The Message*.
9. Dorothy Sayers, *Letters to a Diminished Church: Passionate Arguments for the Relevance of Christian Doctrine* (Nashville: Thomas Nelson, 2004), 4.
10. Eugene H. Peterson, "The Cradle" (poem), *Holy Luck* (Grand Rapids: Wm. B. Eerdmans, 2013), 13.

CHAPTER EIGHT: AN UNEXPECTED LEGACY

1. Barbara Brown Taylor, *Learning to Walk in the Dark* (San Francisco: HarperOne, 2014).
2. *The Book of Common Prayer*, (New York: Church Publishing, 1979), 22.
3. Kathleen Norris, *Amazing Grace: A Vocabulary of Faith* (New York: Riverhead Books, 1999).

4. *The Divine Hours* is a series of books published by Doubleday Religion.
5. John Ortberg, *The Life You've Always Wanted* (Grand Rapids, MI: Zondervan, 2002).

CHAPTER NINE: WILD GOOSE
1. Manning, *Relentless Tenderness*, 181.
2. Excerpted from 1 Corinthians 13.
3. http://christianity.about.com/od/denominations/p/christiantoday.htm.
4. Acts 1:8.
5. Acts 2:2–4 NLT.
6. Acts 2: 43–47.
7. Harvey Cox, *Fire From Heaven: The Rise of Pentecostal Spirituality and the Reshaping of Religion in the Twenty-First Century* (Boston: DeCapo Press, 2001).
8. Jack S. Deere, *Surprised by the Power of the Spirit* (Grand Rapids: Zondervan, 1996), 152.
9. Ibid., 191.
10. Gordon Fee, *The First Epistle to the Corinthians, Revised Edition.* (Grand Rapids, MI: Wm. B. Eerdmans, 2014), 375, phrase appears in footnote reference 305.
11. Kelley Nikondeha, *A Deeper Story*, http://deeperstory.com/a-care-ful-charismatic/.
12. Luke 18:1–8.
13. Barbara Kingsolver, *Animal Dreams* (New York: Harper Perrenial Reissue Edition, 2013), 299.
14. Hebrews 11:1, "Now faith is confidence in what we hope for and assurance about what we do not see." (NIV)
15. Galatians 5:22.
16. Acts 5:35–39, NLT.
17. Excerpted from the poem "As Kingfishers Catch Fire," by Gerard Manley Hopkins.
18. Isaiah 43:19a.

CHAPTER TEN: OBEY THE SADNESS
1. Michael Gungor and Lisa Gungor, "When Death Dies," from the album *Ghosts Upon the Earth* (Atlanta: Brash Music, 2011).

2.   Frederick Buechner, *Telling the Truth: The Gospel as Tragedy, Comedy, and Fairy Tale* (Harper & Row, 1977), 15.

3.   Matthew 16:13–20.

4.   Greg Boyd, *Is God to Blame?*, 61.

5.   Ephesians 6:12.

6.   Richard Rohr, *Eager to Love*, 25.

7.   Jeremiah 6:14.

CHAPTER ELEVEN: BEAUTIFUL FACADE

1.   http://www.huffingtonpost.com/2013/03/25/jalousie-slum-painted -psychedelic-colors-haiti-photos_n_2950587.html.

2.   Ken Wytsma, *Pursuing Justice: The Call to Live and Die for Bigger Things* (Nashville: Thomas Nelson, 2013), 9.

3.   Eugene Cho, *Overrated: Are We More in Love with the Idea of Changing the World Than Actually Changing the World* (Colorado Springs: David C. Cook, 2014), 38.

4.   For more on this issue, I wish everyone would read *When Helping Hurts: How to Alleviate Poverty Without Hurting the Poor . . . and Yourself* by Steve Corbett and Brian Fikkert (Chicago: Moody Publishers, 2014)

5.   The *restavek* system is a form of child slave labor. Poor families "sell" their children to wealthier families or institutions in an attempt to secure them an education or a stable source of food and water. However, many of the patrons abuse, starve, and enslave the children. They often work 10–14 hours a day without any pay. This system is one major reason why Haiti is the worst country in the world for child slavery. http://www.businessinsider.com/flawed-arrangement-turns -haitian-restaveks-into-slaves-2014–8.

CHAPTER TWELVE: EVANGELICAL HERO COMPLEX

1.   Thomas C. Oden, *Pastoral Theology: Essentials of Ministry* (San Francisco: Harper, 1983), 88.

2.   Arthur Holmes, *All Truth Is God's Truth* (Downers Grove, Ill. InterVarsity, 1977), 27.

3.   R. Paul Stevens, *The Other Six Days: Vocation, Work, and Ministry in Biblical Perspective* (Grand Rapids, MI: Eerdmans; Vancouver: Regent College, 2000), 5.

4. Ibid.
5. Commenting on Ephesians says, Stevens adds, "If Christ has broken down the dividing wall between Jew and Gentile (surely an awesome miracle, 3:4–6) then it would be anathema to erect a wall between one part of the body and another." 55.
6. Stevens, 32.
7. As taught and demonstrated by Jesus (Mark 10:42–45) and instructed by Peter (1 Peter 5:4).
8. Fee, 7.
9. Richard Rohr, *Eager to Love*, 34.
10. 2 Thess. 1:11.
11. This is a theme throughout much of Brueggemann's work but a good starting point is "Journey to the Common Good."
12. Walter Brueggemann, *Sabbath as Resistance: Saying No to the Culture of Now* (Louisville, KY: Westminster John Knox Press, 2014).

Discussion Questions

✳

NOTE: The questions below are meant to help you sort through your faith—at whatever level and depth you are comfortable. You can think through these questions on your own—perhaps using a journal to gather your thoughts—or you can discuss them with others who are also reading the book. When discussing with others, share what you're ready to share. There may be some things you're not quite ready to sort through yet—and that's perfectly all right.

CHAPTER 1: OUT OF SORTS: A BEGINNING

- Can you think of a time, in any area of your life, when you could relate to Sarah's definition of "out of sorts"—what was getting you "out of sorts," and what did it feel like?
- What fears rise to the surface when you think about that time—or the feeling of being out of sorts?
- In what ways, if any, can you relate to the period of doubting—the wilderness that Sarah describes? What triggered your doubts?
- In what ways have you sorted through grief in the physical world in your own life? Have you confronted the mess of loss and found healing? How did that healing—whether full or partial—come?

CHAPTER 2: THERE'S SOMETHING ABOUT THAT NAME: ON GETTING TO KNOW JESUS

- When was the last time you talked about Jesus—not church, or God, or Christianity, but Jesus? What did the conversation sound like?

- Can you remember what the name "Jesus" meant to you when you first came to know it? Think about a time when you were naive in your understanding of Him.
- How has your understanding of Him changed?
- What counterfeit Jesuses have you come across in your life? How have they affected you?

CHAPTER 3: EVERYONE GETS TO PLAY: ON THEOLOGY AND CHANGE

- What questions of theology have you repeatedly struggled to answer? Do any of Sarah's ring a bell in your life?
- What has your relationship been like with theology? Have you felt welcome to "play" with the big ideas and questions in your life? Have you learned more from scholars or "ordinary" people?
- Do you feel free to ask questions—like a child would—about what you want to know? Maybe you can share one big question that you truly want to find an answer for.

CHAPTER 4: GETTING INTO THE WORD: ON THE BIBLE

- What basic expectations do you have about the Bible? What were you taught to believe about the words of the Bible?
- Are there stories in the Old Testament you find yourself wanting to skip?
- How might those stories be reinterpreted through the lens of the New Testament Jesus?
- Have you been given or taken on a life verse? What is that verse? How has its meaning changed for you over the years?
- What do you love about the Bible and why? The psalms, the promises, the picture of Jesus? Take a minute to share if you can.

CHAPTER 5: THE PEOPLE OF GOD: ON CHURCH

- Can you relate to Sarah's journey through the churches of her past? What has your journey looked like, and where are you now?
- How would you describe your "mother church?" Do you feel a need or desire to remain loyal to that church?
- Are there specific issues with the Church that you struggle to reconcile? Share one of those issues, if you'd like.

- Can you approach your church questions, doubts, or frustrations as a pilgrim on a journey through the wilderness to a place of healing you can't yet see? What would that approach look like?

CHAPTER 6: BE A PERSON: ON COMMUNITY AND FRIENDSHIP

- How have you seen the efforts to foster community in a church fail? How have you seen them succeed?
- What do you seek from community? Can you identify what drives you to need others and what is false pressure from an outside ideal?
- Can you relate to Sarah's idea of concentric circles of relationship? How does this play out in your life?
- Can you identify the "Somewheres" in your life? Have you expressed the importance of those relationships to one another?

CHAPTER 7: TRULY HUMAN: ON HEAVEN AND THE KINGDOM OF GOD

- What do you think of the idea that Sin Management is only the beginning of atonement—that there is real work and transformation in the Gospel of the Kingdom of God? That there is a difference between converts and disciples?
- Do you find yourself focused on the broken and the darkness? Think about where you have seen light and beauty in this world recently— evidence of new life being breathed into death. If you like, share what that light and new life have looked like in your life.
- How can we lean into the Kingdom of God now, and not simply wait for the "yet to come?"

CHAPTER 8: AN UNEXPECTED LEGACY: ON THE ANCIENT PRACTICES

- What seasons of light and darkness—certainty and doubt—have you experienced in your faith? Which is a more natural state for your soul right now?
- Do the traditions of liturgy and spiritual disciplines bring you comfort or intimidate you? What has been your experience with these ancient practices?
- Without being bound by traditional categories of Christians, try to define your unique combination of theological ingredients. What pieces of the

gigantic pie do you desire and need to feel alive in your faith—to see and hold onto Jesus?

CHAPTER 9: WILD GOOSE: ON FAITH, THE SPIRIT, SIGNS, AND WONDERS

* What is your relationship with the mystical elements of faith, such as the gift of speaking in tongues?
* Is it easy for you to accept the breadth of believers—in all their different shapes and sizes—around the world? Or do you struggle to embrace the disparities of worship and understanding in the wider family of Christian brothers and sisters? You might share a little about where you are.
* How do you pray? With a goal? With a candle? In murmurs throughout your day or at an altar on Sunday?
* How do you reconcile faith and the complicated reality of answered and unanswered prayers?

CHAPTER 10: OBEY THE SADNESS: ON GRIEF AND LAMENT

* How do you face grief and sadness when it comes? Do you compartmentalize the pain?
* What were you taught about darkness and pain in your church tradition? What do you believe now about its place in your faith?
* When bad things happen, are you tempted to look for someone to blame—yourself? God?
* What would it look like for us to truly lament in a time of loss and sadness instead of rushing to platitudes and talking points for comfort?

CHAPTER 11: BEAUTIFUL FACADE: ON JUSTICE AND SHALOM

* What big feelings rise up in you when the conversation turns to justice?
* Is it a new idea to think of joining the work God is already doing in a place of need or injustice? What if the mission trip is bringing God to a place, while being a part of what He's already doing there?
* Do you believe you can move mountains through small acts of revolution in your own kitchen . . . small town . . . life? Through acts of kindness . . . hope . . . love? Any experiences you'd like to share?

CHAPTER 12: EVANGELICAL HERO COMPLEX:
ON VOCATION AND CALLING

- Have you experienced the "evangelical hero complex" in your own life? Or the hero worship of others doing big things for God?
- Can you really accept and believe that you can be a carpenter or a banker or a teacher or a mom for the glory of God? How has that been confirmed or denied in your life?
- What if there were no divisions of the sacred and secular in your life? How would your life look different?
- Is there a difference for you in being "used by God" and being "loved by God"? Can you put your finger on the paradigm shift?

BENEDICTION

- How is it there, in the wilderness? Are you growing more comfortable in your wandering, in this process of sorting?
- What do you feel you need to continue this hard work? Courage? Imagination? Community? Space to grieve? How can your Somewheres support and pray for you?

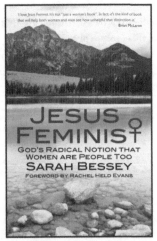